What's Prayer Got To Do With It?

A faithful journey of Scriptural prayers—
A prayerful journey of Scriptural faith

Beth Armstrong

What's Prayer Got To Do With It?
A faithful journey of Scriptural prayers—
A prayerful journey of Scriptural faith
by Beth Armstrong

Printed in the United States of America

ISBN 978-1-60647-945-2

www.xulonpress.com

To Caleb and Quinn,

I ask God to strengthen you by His Spirit. . . that Christ will live in you as you open the door and invite Him in. And I ask God that with both feet planted firmly on love, you'll be able to take in the extravagant dimensions of Christ's love. Reach out and experience the breadth! Test its length! Plumb the depths! Rise to the heights! Live full lives, full in the fullness of God.

(Adapted from Ephesians 3:16-19, The Message)

Contents

Introduction

Nobody reads these introductions. Well. . . let me clarify. I shouldn't say *nobody*. I should say *most* don't. Most people don't read the introduction, preface, forward, acknowledgements, or anything else that comes before page one, chapter one. They just dive right in.

Obviously if you're still reading you're not one of those people. Thanks, by the way.

The birth of a book is sometimes interesting to certain people and otherwise boring for others. I thought I'd share briefly how this one came into being for those who are interested.

In the summer of 2005 our church was teaching seven key elements of discipleship. Prayer was one of those elements and I was asked to teach one Sunday on this subject of prayer. Since prayer is my passion, perhaps some of my giftedness, and simply how God has wired me, I was flattered and jumped at the opportunity. After the class several people came up and commented that I was speaking directly to them, that everything I said resonated with them, and they were challenged in ways they hadn't been challenged before. One of my dear friends even pulled me aside in another room after class and said, "Beth you should teach an entire unit on prayer. You should teach our church more about this thing called prayer."

So, by September I found myself teaching a class that I chose to call "Devoted to Prayer." Only there was no book. There was no curriculum. No guidelines. No syllabus. How does one teach a class on prayer without a curriculum? You go directly to the source. . . the Word of God. I began studying the numerous prayers of the Bible and God began to formulate in my mind what a class on prayer would look like. I studied each prayer and asked myself the questions, "What does this specific prayer have to do with me? What does this specific prayer have to do with me and my circumstances? What does this specific prayer have to do with me and my life?"

That's how the class happened. Each week we looked at a different prayer of the Bible. We looked at the circumstances surrounding that prayer. Who prayed it? Why? And what does God want us to learn and apply from studying that prayer?

After the class ended in December, I had several people approach me with the idea of writing a book based on the curriculum I wrote to teach the class. And my immediate response to them was, "Are you nuts? Do you know how much time and effort goes into writing a book?"

Well, time, effort, blood, (well. . . maybe not blood), sweat, tears, and lots of prayer have resulted in the book you now hold in your hands.

That's how it happened. It's a gift from my class. It's a message from my heart. In the chapters that follow we'll look at numerous prayers spoken by men and women in the Bible dealing with different circumstances of life. We'll take a close look at those circumstances, the prayers they prayed, and what we can learn and apply in our own lives. My hope is that everyone from the novice to the seasoned prayer veteran will be challenged in their own life of prayer and knowledge of God's Word.

Blessings to you—for reading the introduction—and for joining me on a journey to discover *What's Prayer Got To Do With It?*

1

Making Our Busyness Our Business
(Matthew 6:5-9a)

When was the last time you prayed? No, I mean *really* prayed. Not the kind of prayer that is said at mealtime or at bedtime with your kids. Not the kind of desperation prayer that is said right before you take a test for which you haven't studied sufficiently, or the kind you say after you speed past a parked policeman with a radar gun. But the kind of prayer that is just *you* and *God*. . . sitting alone. . . quietly . . . with no distractions. . . you talking, Him listening. . . and vice versa. When was the last time you prayed like that?

Some of you might say, "I don't know how to pray like that." (I hope to change that response by the end of the book.) Others may say, "A prayer is a prayer is a prayer. What's the difference? As long as I'm praying, that's all that matters." (I hope to transform that one, too.) And then there are those who might simply say, "I'm just too busy to pray like that."

I was enjoying breakfast with my sons before school a few years ago. Quinn (then six years old) said, "Mom, do you know what I wish? I wish I could take my bike to school and ride it all over the playground, the parking lot, the school yard anytime and anywhere I wanted."

"Well," I responded, "they probably have rules about that."

"Why, mom?"

"Quinn, think about it," I explained. "If every kid wanted to take their bike to school and ride it all over the playground, parking lot, school yard anytime and anywhere they wanted, it would be total chaos!"

"So?" Quinn said quite confidently. "I love chaos!"

Caleb (my older son) and I laughed out loud at his comment. Within seconds, Quinn responded, "By the way, mom. . . what is chaos?"

I went on to explain to my young son that in simple terms chaos was the absence of peace. The absence of order. The absence of silence. And unfortunately this is how we live our lives—in the absence of peace, order, and silence. In our busyness we have gotten so caught up in doing that we fail to stop and behold the face of Jesus.

WHAT PRAYER IS

Busyness. That's what I want to address in this chapter— the "I'm too busy to pray" response. But, before we go any further, let's take a look at what prayer is and what it's not. Read these thoughts on prayer from several well known people:

> Prayer is not asking. It is a longing of the soul. It is daily admission of one's weakness... It is better in prayer to have a heart without words than words without a heart.
>
> - Gandhi[1]

Real prayer…is realistic, spontaneous, down-to-earth communication with the living Lord that results in a relief of personal anxiety and a calm assurance that our God is in full control of our circumstances.

- Chuck Swindoll[2]

Of all the Spiritual Disciplines prayer is the most central because it ushers us into perpetual communion with the Father… Real prayer is life creating and life changing.

- Richard Foster[3]

Prayer is much more than just giving a list of desires to God… Prayer is acknowledging and experiencing the presence of God and inviting His presence into our lives and circumstances. It's seeking the presence of God and releasing the power of God which gives us the means to overcome any problem.

- Stormie Omartian[4]

These are all accurate thoughts and definitions of what prayer *is*. I even have my own definition of prayer: Prayer is the privilege we have to draw near to the heart of God—both speaking to and hearing from our gracious Heavenly Father. I call it a privilege because I truly believe that the means to communicate with the God who created the entire universe and created me is a gift. It's an honor, and a pleasure, and a joy. We *get* to pray! God could have created the world and all its people then said, "See ya' later, you're on your own." But He didn't! He stuck around because He loves to have fellowship with His created beings. My experience has been that as God loves to hear from me, He also loves to communicate back. . . if I'm open and willing.

WHAT PRAYER IS NOT

Sometimes, in order to gain an understanding of what something is, it is helpful to look at what it's not. Hear the words from Jesus' Sermon on the Mount in the Gospel of Matthew, according to Eugene Peterson's translation of the Bible called *The Message*:

> [5]And when you come before God, don't turn that into a theatrical production either. All these people making a regular show out of their prayers, hoping for stardom! Do you think God sits in a box seat?
>
> [6]Here's what I want you to do: Find a quiet, secluded place so you won't be tempted to role-play before God. Just be there as simply and honestly as you can manage. The focus will shift from you to God, and you will begin to sense his grace.
>
> [7]The world is full of so-called prayer warriors who are prayer-ignorant. They're full of formulas and programs and advice, peddling techniques for getting what you want from God. [8]Don't fall for that nonsense. This is your Father you are dealing with, and he knows better than you what you need. [9]With a God like this loving you, you can pray very simply.
>
> (Matthew 6:5-9a)

From these five verses we gain several insights into what prayer is not. *First, prayer is not a theatrical production (v. 5).* This verse is referring to the hypocrites of Jesus' day who, while praying in the synagogues and street corners, loved to pray "to be seen by men." The Contemporary English Version refers to them as "show-offs." Peterson points out that these hypocrites were making a regular show out of their prayers, hoping for stardom! They brought attention to themselves by their award winning theatrical performances. Since when is prayer about performing for others? So, in fact, the hypocrites weren't really talking to God at all.

Second, prayer is not role-playing before God (v. 6). How often do we act like someone we're not when other people are around? We often try to impress our bosses, neighbors, and even church friends. We fake our compassion, our sincerity, or even our strength in an effort to hide who we really are on the inside. But when we pray, we cannot hide anything from God. We cannot pretend to be something we are not. We can't pull the wool over His eyes, because He's God. He created us. He knows us. He sees right through our superficiality and peers directly into our hearts. We cannot role-play before the Almighty God.

Third, prayer is not focused on me (v. 6). Rick Warren's book, *The Purpose Driven Life*, opens with this sentence: "It's not about you!"[5] Life is not about you. Despite what TV, radio, billboards, therapy, and society screams these days, life is not about you. Similarly, prayer is not about you either. It's not our opportunity to go air out our dirty laundry. It's not our chance to place our order to the voice on the other end of the drive-through mechanism, only to have what we want delivered to our window in a matter of minutes. Remember what Stormie Omartian said in her definition of prayer: "It is acknowledging and experiencing the presence of God..." To acknowledge means to admit or accept that something is true, to show awareness of something, or to show appreciation. We cannot truly acknowledge God in an acceptable way when our hearts and minds are stuck on us. After all, prayer is relational. It's about the relationship between God and us.

Finally, prayer is not a formula, a program, or a technique (v. 7). When we pray rote prayers, we check our hearts at the door and rely solely on our minds to pray for us. But when we shift our thinking on prayer from human principles to pouring our hearts out before Him, we discover not only the true essence of prayer, but the freedom we have therein. Following a formula restrains the Spirit of God within us. We begin to pray out of obligation; we're just going through the motions. Prayer shouldn't be merely our duty—it should be our delight! It shouldn't be solely our job—it should be our joy!

THE TEMPORARILY MISPLACED PRIVILEGE

When we are too busy to pray, we miss out on that pleasure, delight, and joy that God has in store for us! He longs to commune with us. He longs to spend time with us. And truthfully, my heart aches for all of God's children who have "temporarily misplaced" the privilege they have of drawing near to the throne of grace.

So, how busy are you? Stop for a moment and ponder that question. Ask yourself, "How busy *am* I?" Let's try a little exercise. Grab a piece of paper and a pencil and think about your typical week, day by day. I would ask you to do this mentally, but there is something powerful about seeing it on paper. Jot down the activities, commitments, involvements, duties, and responsibilities that comprise each day of your week. Start with Sunday, end with Saturday, and make a complete list. Be specific, writing down times and places of events. For example, one of your days may look something like this:

6 a.m. - wake up and get ready
7 a.m. – 7:45 a.m. - get everyone ready and out the door
8 a.m. – 5 p.m. - work
5 p.m. – 5:30 p.m. - help kids with homework
5:30 p.m. – 6:30 p.m. - make/eat dinner
7 p.m. - take child #1 to piano lessons
7:30 p.m. – take child #2 to karate
8 p.m. - pick up child #1 from piano

18

8:30 p.m. - pick up child #2 from karate
9 p.m. - get kids ready for bed
9:30 p.m. - put kids to bed
10 p.m. - get ready for bed
10:30 p.m. - collapse!

And that was just a typical Monday! I don't know about you, but I'm worn out already, and there are still six more days in the week.

Glance back over the list you just made. Have you left anything out? Add it in. Be sure you are making a thorough and *honest* analysis of each day in your normal week.

Is your list a short one? Perhaps you have only a few activities a couple times a week. Good for you! Or perhaps your list is quite lengthy. Is your day-to-day list of commitments and responsibilities a mile long? Or maybe *miles* long? Is your typical week beginning to resemble the Boston marathon? Your schedule may look quite different than the example above, and that's ok. But in principle, I think you'll agree that most people are over extended in their busyness.

You can laugh that off and find humor in your "never-a-dull-moment life." But I hope you don't. Bill Hybels, pastor at Willowcreek Church, wrote a book some years ago entitled *Too Busy Not to Pray*. (The title itself speaks volumes, doesn't it?) He suggests this thought: "Never a *dull* moment; never a *reflective* moment either."[6] There is real truth (and sorrow) in that statement, isn't there? If, in our busyness, we never pause to reflect on our Creator, His plan for our lives, what He wants us to do and be, then we're missing out on the most valuable relationship we can ever have.

We are busy people! Face it. Busyness is what is accepted, what is demanded, and what has become the norm. We are committed over here, pulled over there, stretched in this way, and involved in that way. I'll say it again: We are busy people!

THE CHOICE OF A COMPLICATED LIFE

Hear the words from Ecclesiastes 7:29 in the Good News (Today's English Version) Bible, "God made us plain and simple, but we have made ourselves very complicated." Sometimes our busyness is a *season* of life. And sometimes it is a *choice* of life. We have chosen to make ourselves complicated. We'd never admit that our lives were complicated because that has such a negative connotation. It indicates that our lives are difficult to understand or deal with. But at the same time, we have chosen to be full of activity, always on the go, fully engaged in too many activities.

No wonder, then, many people respond to the question that opened this chapter by saying, "I'm just too busy to pray like that." If we are too busy to pray like that, then where does God fit into our fast-paced lives? If we are too busy to pray like that, then how do we allow God to guide and direct us, to teach us, to mold and fashion us into the likeness of His Son? Furthermore, if we are not spending time nurturing our relationship with our Heavenly Father, then how do we live our lives as genuine followers of Christ?

Isn't it true that we make time for those things that are important to us? Think about it. If I really want to know everything there is to know about Abraham Lincoln, for example, then I will set aside great amounts of time to read and study and understand Abraham Lincoln. Eventually, with time and diligence, I'll become an expert on the sixteenth President of the United States.

Similarly, if I truly want to learn to play tennis, I'll digest a rule book on the sport, watch a lot of tennis on television, and spend an abundance of time on the courts practicing. With time and effort (and a lot of sweat), I'll be ready to take on Venus or Serena Williams.

The key ingredient in achieving this type of success, or rating, or status, is *time*. And although we will never be "experts" in following Christ, and we will never be ready to "take on" the Apostles Paul or Peter, we can become more intimate in our walk with Jesus if we choose to spend the time.

PRAYERS FALLING PREY

The chief rival of time is busyness. We frequently catch ourselves saying, "I wish I had more time to do _____ _____ (fill in the blank), but I can't seem to find it." The fact is that our time has been devoured. It has fallen prey to the demands of the world.

Given the opportunity, I think many people would categorically say, "I wish I had more time in my day to spend with God." Or, "If I had more time, I would read my Bible more." Maybe even, "There are so many people and situations I need to be praying for, but I just don't have the time."

Chuck Swindoll, in his book *Intimacy with the Almighty*, has "found that there are at least four essential decisions, each related to a discipline, that assist us in cultivating an in-depth intimacy with the Almighty."[7] According to Swindoll, those four essential decisions are: reorder your private world, be still, cultivate serenity, and trust the Lord completely. Along with those decisions come four disciplines: simplicity, silence, solitude, and surrender.

If we long to be genuine followers of Christ, it is essential to restructure our busyness. We must simplify our frazzled, over-committed lives. We must incorporate moments of stillness and quiet before the Lord. And we must carve out times of solitude when nobody else is around to interrupt our precious appointment with our Creator.

God is not an "on-the-go" type of God who is satisfied with our meeting Him as we are coming and going. He is worthy of more than our quick fixes and leftovers. He deserves more than our spare time.

Remember, prayer is the *privilege* we have to draw near to the heart of God, both speaking to and hearing from our gracious Heavenly Father. We don't have to pray—we *get* to pray! Recall that Richard Foster put it this way, "Real prayer is life creating and life changing." Wouldn't it be great if all Christians experienced this type of prayer?

Maybe you are already experiencing that type of prayer in your life. To those folks I rejoice with you and say a hearty, "Hallelujah!" But maybe you are not experiencing anything close to "life creating and life changing." Maybe your prayer life is uneventful, flat, boring, or even nonexistent.

We are about to embark on a journey that I hope will not only enlighten and strengthen your life of prayer, but will challenge you to new heights in your walk with Jesus Christ. Because of this thing we call prayer, many people's lives in both the Old and New Testaments were changed forever. They saw God reveal Himself in magnificent ways because they grasped the privilege of drawing near to the heart of God—because they prayed!

MAKING IT REAL

1. How would you respond to the following statement: I am too busy right now to have a quality quiet time regularly. True or false?
2. What part does your pride play in your busyness?
3. Richard Foster said "Real prayer is life creating and life changing." Is that something you are currently experiencing in your prayer life? If not, why not? What might it take on your part to experience this kind of prayer?
4. How does your belief in God affect your prayers? (i.e. Big God, big prayers. Distant God, distant prayers.)

5. Do you honestly long to be a genuine follower of Jesus Christ? What are you willing to do that will start you on your journey?

2

I Surrender All
(Matthew 26:36-44)

Control freaks. Do you know any of those? I ran across a list of "Characteristics of the Control Freak" recently. See if any of these behaviors sound familiar.

The control freak:

- Is described by most people as picky and critical, as well as controlling.
- Loves order and established routines. Don't even think about touching things on his or her desk. Watch out if his or her plans have to be rearranged.
- Always needs to be right.
- Tells you who you are and what you think.
- Implies that you're wrong or inadequate when you don't agree.
- Would rather give orders than take them.
- Feels most comfortable when in charge.
- Believes winning an argument is more important than finding the best solution.[1]

Maybe those characteristics sound all too familiar because you work for a control freak. Maybe you are married to one or grew up having a parent who was a control freak. Or it just might be possible that you greet one every morning as you look in the mirror.

What is it about control that we crave? For many, control equals power, authority, dominance, influence, strength, clout, muscle, and ability. Even if we are not control freaks, per se, there are definitely things in our lives that we like to exercise power or authority over. For example, we like to be in command of things such as our finances, our career path, our weekend plans, vacation plans, etc. We even think we have a need to be in charge of our pasts, our addictions, our health, the people in our lives, and our futures.

I was blown away by something I read not long ago. It was an article that came from the Aircraft Owners and Pilots Association entitled "Control Freaks." The article offered advice to people who are learning to fly. Here's what it said: "If a pilot doesn't learn early in training that an airplane, given half a chance, will do most of the work once level flight has been established, he or she may be doomed to a career of needless fiddling with the controls; excessive fatigue; and a stable of reluctant, unhappy, even airsick passengers. It's almost too simple to be true, but as instructional advice goes, 'Let go' can be the best advice some pilots ever receive."[2]

Isn't that interesting? The two most significant words that a flight instructor can say to a student pilot who is just beginning to learn how an airplane flies are, "Let go." *Let go*! Those two words alone are enough to send us into orbit. Some of you are thinking about your own circumstances and responding, "Let go? Are you nuts? There's no way I could do that!"

OBSTACLES TO OVERCOME

What things in your life do you like to control? What things in your life do you like to be in charge of and/or manage to the extent of denying God His rightful place on the throne of your life? What areas of your life are you unwilling to yield to God because "letting go" would be too frightening?

Letting go is a form of surrender. And the opposite of surrender is control. Unfortunately, we have come to believe that surrender (in its negative context) is synonymous with words such as weakness, powerlessness, helplessness, inability, and vulnerability. I view surrender as a willingness to yield to something greater than myself. It's a choice I make that conveys I don't know best in a particular situation, therefore I will yield to those who do. It's not an easy choice. But most of the time, it's a wise one.

What gets in the way of us surrendering those areas of our lives to God? What are the obstacles we cannot seem to overcome when faced with relinquishing our desire for control over to God? See if you can relate to this partial list:

- *Fear of the unknown.* "I don't know what will happen if I let God have this particular area of my life. What if I fall flat on my face?"
- *Fear of being found out.* "What if people find out that I have a problem? What will they think if I need to go to counseling for this issue? I don't want to ask for help because that will appear that I am weak. My reputation is much too important."
- *Pride.* "I can handle this. I'm smart, I'm wealthy, I'm healthy, etc. I don't need anyone's help or advice. I have gotten myself out of plenty of jams before, I can do it again." (Pride, when it's all said and done isn't about arrogance or conceit. It's about control!)

- *A comfort zone issue.* "I don't want to risk the embarrassment, awkwardness, or even confrontation that surrendering might lead to. That would be much too uncomfortable for me. I'm very comfortable where I am."
- *Lack of desire.* "I flat out don't want to allow God access to this particular part of my life. I like controlling it. I do a great job of it on my own. Besides, if I let God take control of this area of my life, that might mean I have to change, and I like me just the way I am."
- *It's too big of a burden for God.* "God doesn't care about this one little issue in my life. He's too busy fixing all the big problems. OR... I've gotten myself in such a mess, there's no way God could fix all of it."

If we know the promises of God and firmly believe them, then why do we fail to relinquish control of our lives (or at least certain parts of it) to God? Jeremiah 29:11 reads, "'For I know the plans I have for you,' declares the LORD, 'plans to prosper you and not to harm you, plans to give you hope and a future.'" God's plans and purposes are sovereign (Isaiah 46:9-11). His plans are supreme, superior, and absolute. Within the word sovereign is the smaller word "reign." It serves as a reminder to us what the word sovereign means. Simply put, God reigns. If we believe in the sovereignty of God, then the most appropriate response for us as devoted followers of Christ is to surrender our whole lives to Him.

That's what Jesus did.

"That was easy!" you might say, "because Jesus *was* God." Do you honestly think it was *easy* for the Son of God to "let go"? Was it really *easy* for Jesus to surrender? If it was easy, Jesus would be less human than He was God. And we know that Jesus was fully human. In His humanity He actually struggled just like you and me. I take great comfort knowing we have a God who cared so much about us that He sent His Son to earth to experience everything we experience.

THE SURRENDER OF THE SAVIOR

Right before Jesus was arrested, He took the Disciples to the Garden of Gethsemane to pray. Here is the account:

> [36]Then Jesus went with his disciples to a place called Gethsemane, and he said to them, "Sit here while I go over there and pray." [37]He took Peter and the two sons of Zebedee along with him, and he began to be sorrowful and troubled. [38]Then he said to them, "My soul is overwhelmed with sorrow to the point of death. Stay here and keep watch with me."
>
> [39]Going a little farther, he fell with his face to the ground and prayed, "My Father, if it is possible, may this cup be taken from me. Yet not as I will, but as you will."
>
> [40]Then he returned to his disciples and found them sleeping. "Could you men not keep watch with me for one hour?" he asked Peter. [41]"Watch and pray so that you will not fall into temptation. The spirit is willing, but the body is weak."
>
> [42]He went away a second time and prayed, "My Father, if it is not possible for this cup to be taken away unless I drink it, may your will be done."
>
> [43]When he came back, he again found them sleeping, because their eyes were heavy. [44]So he left them and went away once more and prayed the third time, saying the same thing.
>
> (Matthew 26:36-44)

This is actually a loaded passage of Scripture. We could learn many lessons from this passage alone. But I want to dissect Jesus' prayer and apply it to our own experience of prayer.

At this stage in Jesus' life, He was about to be arrested and shortly thereafter crucified. His death was imminent. He had predicted His death and informed His disciples (Matthew 16:21, Matthew 20:17-19). Can you imagine what our Lord must have been feeling? We don't have to imagine long, because we see the display of His emotions here in this passage.

LESSONS FROM OUR LORD

As Jesus prays, we see four different aspects that not only teach us about who He is, but also teach us vital lessons about prayer.

First, we see the humanity of Jesus. Verse 37 reads, "He began to be sorrowful and troubled." The New American Standard Version acknowledges that Jesus began to be "grieved and distressed." Jesus, being fully human and fully God, was overwhelmed. There was no hiding His emotions. There was no burying the anguish He felt. He shared this with Peter, James, and John before going to His Heavenly Father in prayer.

We don't need to hide our emotions either. We don't need to bury deep within us the sorrow, or grief, or distress we feel before we spend time in prayer. We don't need to approach God with poker faces or even without our mascara running down our faces. He knows what we're feeling anyway. For "nothing in all creation is hidden from God's sight..." (Hebrews 4:13a).

Second, we see the desperation of Jesus. Jesus, whose soul is crushed with grief, fell face down on the ground and prayed. Maybe His whole body was weakened by His anguish. Or maybe His only response to His troubled soul was to fall before His Father. By falling, by bowing, by lying prostrate we position ourselves correctly before our God. I don't mean to indicate that falling face down in prayer to God is the *only* way to pray. It's one way. Being face down is an outward expression of what's taking place on the inside. It's a reflection of a humbled heart yielded to an amazing God.

Have you ever been in a desperate situation? Have you ever been so worried, so anxious, so fraught with emotion? Take a lesson from the Master and, in your desperation, fall face down in prayer before God.

Third, we see the desire of Jesus. There is so much more to prayer than giving God a list of our desires. But in this situation, Jesus brought His one and only desire before God in prayer. Not once. Not twice. But three times Jesus prayed, "If it is possible, may this cup be taken from me." He prayed that "if it were possible, the awful hour awaiting him might pass him by" (Mark 14:35, NLT). Jesus' longing was that He wouldn't have to go through what He already knew He'd have to go through.

Praying our desires is certainly a part of prayer. "The Lord longs to be gracious to you; He rises to show you compassion" (Isaiah 30:18a). We have a gracious Heavenly Father who wants to bless us and give us the desires of our hearts. Unfortunately, the desires of our hearts are not always in agreement with His good and perfect will. In Jesus' case, His desire to have the cup taken from Him was not part of God's perfect plan. And isn't that a reason to rejoice?

Finally, we see the surrender of Jesus. Though Jesus prayed three times that He wouldn't have to go through the upcoming excruciating events, He also added, "yet not as I will, but as you will." "I want your will, not mine" (v. 39b, NLT). Despite Jesus' desire, He ultimately surrendered His own will to that of His Father. Jesus knew that He was in the hands of the Almighty God. What better place was there for Him to be? He knew that God's plan was not only better, but it was perfect.

THE MOST FRIGHTENING AND MOST POWERFUL PRAYER

"May Your will be done" (v. 42b). That very prayer is perhaps the most *frightening* and most *powerful* prayer we can pray! It is frightening because we might not get our way. It is frightening because God's will is still unknown—albeit good, pleasing, and perfect, it is still out of our control. His will might appear too hard for us or even call us out of our comfort zones. And I don't know about you, but being outside of my comfort zone can terrify me.

It is powerful because we are stepping out of the way and finally letting God be God. When we stop controlling the many aspects of our lives and let God take over, He can finally accomplish His purposes through us. God will do great things in us and through us if we will only let Him.

I frequently say that my biggest stumbling block to spiritual growth and maturity is that I have too much of me in me. I am the one who gets in the way of God really accomplishing great things in me or through me. My pride, my fear, my doubt, my lack of desire—all these things take up residence in me to the degree that there is little room for God to work. As John the Baptist said in John 3:30 "He must increase, but I must decrease" (NAS). The Message translation of that same verse reads "This is the assigned moment for Him to move into the center, while I slip off to the sidelines." I love that! If only all God's people would have the same attitude as John the Baptist and put it into practice.

PLAYING GOD

In 2003 Jim Carrey starred in a movie called *Bruce Almighty*. Bruce, played by Carrey, is a bit of an unorthodox news reporter who has his sights set on becoming a news anchor. He has a girlfriend of many years named Grace, who works at the local daycare. Grace loves Bruce and is ready to marry him if he would only ask. But Bruce, being quite self-absorbed, is clueless to Grace's desire.

Through a series of events, Bruce loses his job as a news reporter and meets up face-to-face with God. God says to Bruce, "You've done a lot of complaining about Me and I'm tired of it. You think you can do My job better than Me, so here's your chance. I'm offering you My job." So God goes on vacation and Bruce becomes "God." He has every power that God has, but he cannot mess with free will or let anyone know that he is God.

As you might imagine, Bruce literally makes a mess of things. Not only does he mess up his life and Grace's life, but he makes a mess of his community and the world. Upon this realization, he cries out to God in desperation saying, "You win! I'm done! Please. . . I don't want to do this anymore. I don't want to be God. I want You to decide what's right for me. I surrender to Your will." This moment is the climax of the movie and a defining moment in Bruce's life.

Like Bruce, we all love to assume the role of God. We do it without even thinking. And like Bruce, when we get caught up in the power and control, we quickly lose objectivity and create messes in many aspects of our lives. Overall, the movie is a powerful reflection of our desire to *play* God accompanied with the compelling realization that we instead *need* God.

What does it take for us to reach that point? The realization that we aren't God, yet we desperately need Him. What does it take to push us to the edge of the cliff of surrender?

BABY STEPS TO SURRENDER

I heard someone say once that if you are ninety-five percent devoted to God (which is a lot), you are still five percent short. What does it take to get the remaining five percent?

I wish I had the fool-proof surrender method, but I don't. What I will offer are a few "baby steps" to surrender. There are four baby steps to surrendering our control lodged within these verses of God's Word:

> ¹Therefore, since we are surrounded by such a huge crowd of witnesses to the life of faith, let us strip off every weight that slows us down, especially the sin that so easily hinders our progress. And let us run with endurance the race that God has set before us. ²We do this by keeping our eyes on Jesus, on whom our faith depends from start to finish. He was willing to die a shameful death on the cross because of the joy he knew would be his afterward. Now he is seated in the place of highest honor beside God's throne in heaven. ³Think about all he endured when sinful people did such terrible things to him, so that you don't become weary and give up.
>
> (Hebrews 12:1-3, NLT)

The first step to surrendering our control is to strip off every weight that slows us down (v. 1). Whatever is slowing you down. . . get rid of it. What is standing in the way of you being all God wants you to be? Pride, fear, doubt, lack of desire? Rid yourself of those things. They are heavy, a burden, and a mass that is slowing you down. Ask God to help you identify and free you of those things. Study what God's Word has to say about such hindrances as I mentioned above. Ask some friends within the body of Christ to help you and hold you accountable. All too often we're easily convinced (and deceived) that we can fix our own problems. Don't be. God, His Word, and our brothers and sisters in Christ are the best resources. Use them.

The second step to surrendering our control is to run with endurance the race that God has set before us (v. 1). Whose race? Is it our race? Do we get to pick our course? No, it is God's race. It is so important for us to let go of the idea that it's our race to run. The race He has set before us isn't necessarily one paved with completely smooth pathways. No, the race God has set before us contains bumpy roads, some steep grades, a few valleys, maybe a mountain or two, some curves, and a slippery surface, accompanied by smooth roads now and then.

Nobody ever said the journey of a devoted follower of Christ was an easy one. And as crazy as it sounds, I wouldn't prefer it to be easy. I don't know who coined the common phrase "no pain, no gain." But I believe it applies to us regarding our spiritual growth. Our faith will never grow without being challenged. God has intentionally set before us many challenges in the road He's laid out for us. Remember, He's sovereign. So, realizing it is in fact God's race, run it with endurance. Stay the course. Persevere.

The third step to surrender is to keep our eyes on Jesus (v. 2). The NIV reads "let us fix our eyes on Jesus." The word "fix" in the Greek denotes turning the eyes away from other things and fixing them on something else.

As I was reading this passage of Scripture one evening in bed, my youngest son, Quinn (six years old at the time), came in and asked me what I was reading. So, I showed him. The part in my Bible that reads "fix our eyes on Jesus" was highlighted in bright pink and underlined in black. Initially, this just fascinated him because I had written in a book and he knows that writing in his books is "not a good choice."

35

Trying to act interested (which was perhaps an excuse to avoid bedtime), he asked me what that phrase meant. So, as best as I could, I described the meaning of that phrase in six-year-old terms. I said that my goal was to be so much like Jesus that I consistently want to keep my eyes and thoughts on Him. The more I look upon Jesus and study Jesus, the more I will become like Him.

Confused, he looked at me and responded, "But why, mom? Why do you want to be like Jesus? Jesus was a boy!"

I tried to salvage that conversation to no avail. So, I kissed my son and sent him off to bed. But as I reflected on my "six-year-old" definition of "fixing my eyes on Jesus," I thought I hadn't done half bad. I *do* want Jesus to be my focus and the center point of my thoughts. And I know the more I practice, I will become more and more like Christ.

The last step to surrender is to think about all He endured . . . so that we don't become weary and give up (v. 3). Jesus Christ was asked to do far more than we will ever be asked to do. When we compare our circumstances to that of Jesus, there is no question as to who went through the bigger struggle. And He endured all of it for you and me!

I believe if we would embrace these four baby steps, we would open the door to the possibility of truly saying, "May Your will be done."

VICTORY IS IN STORE

With surrender, comes victory! The greater the struggle to surrender, the greater the victory! Think about it. If it isn't very hard for you to surrender your control of something, then your victory is a small one. The reward isn't very sweet if you didn't even have to work at it. But if there is a major issue in your life that you are absolutely struggling to surrender to God, when you ultimately "let go" and allow

God to take control, He is going to honor your obedience to Him and pour out His blessing upon you.

For Christians, some say that the victory for us was won at the Cross. Others say that the victory was won at the empty tomb. But I say that the victory for Christians was won at Gethsemane where Jesus, crying out to God in prayer, surrendered His will to the Father. The victory for us was won when Jesus prayed, "I will do it Your way!" Had He not done that, life for you and me would be vastly (and eternally) different!

Surrender! Let go! Allow God access to every part of you that you want to control . . . and watch Him go to work!

MAKING IT REAL

1. What are the areas of your life where you want to maintain control? What area(s) are you currently struggling to surrender to what God wants for you? Make a list.

2. In the movie *Bruce Almighty*, Bruce makes a real mess of things when he tries to "play God." Can you relate? Have there been similar times in your life when assuming the role of God has made things worse not better?

3. Why is it so easy to give up on the things that God calls us to do? What is it that hinders you from running the race with perseverance?

4. This week make it your goal, your commitment, your priority, your purpose, and your objective to "fix your eyes on Jesus." Be intentional. Be practical. Place note cards or sticky notes on your bathroom mirror, dashboard, microwave, etc. to remind your eyes where they need to be fixed.

3

Mirror, Mirror On The Wall
(Psalm 51:1-17)

Ponder this past week of your life. Consider yourself for a moment—your thoughts, motives, actions, reactions, behaviors, and words. Have you lived a perfectly sinless life in the last week? I recently heard a pastor on television say he was so busy working for the Lord that he didn't have time to sin. (Oh brother! I rolled my eyes, shook my head and thought to myself, "Did he really say that he didn't have time to sin?")

On a scale of one to ten—one being totally sinful, ten being perfect—where would you score yourself based on your performance of the last week? What score would your closest friends give you based on how you have acted around or toward them this past week?

If the truth were known none of us (not even that busy pastor on television) could ever receive a perfect ten. Some weeks we feel pretty good about ourselves and our minimal degree of sinfulness. Perhaps we might rank ourselves an eight or nine. Other weeks we know we have totally blown it. And sadly, we see our score plummet into the abyss of one or two.

ROTTEN THROUGH AND THROUGH

The Apostle Paul, author of several books in the New Testament, said this about his own sinfulness:

> [15]I don't understand myself at all, for I really want to do what is right, but I don't do it. Instead, I do the very thing I hate. [16]I know perfectly well that what I am doing is wrong, and my bad conscience shows that I agree that the law is good. [17]But I can't help myself, because it is sin inside me that makes me do these evil things.
>
> [18]I know I am rotten through and through so far as my old sinful nature is concerned. No matter which way I turn, I can't make myself do right. I want to, but I can't. [19]When I want to do good, I don't. And when I try not to do wrong, I do it anyway. [20]But if I am doing what I don't want to do, I am not really the one doing it; the sin within me is doing it.
>
> [21]It seems to be a fact of life that when I want to do what is right, I inevitably do what is wrong. [22]I love God's law with all my heart. [23]But there is another law at work within me that is at war with my mind. This law wins the fight and makes me a slave to the sin that is still within me. [24]Oh, what a miserable person I am!
>
> (Romans 7:15-24a, NLT)

Can you believe what he is saying about himself? Do you know how good of a guy Paul was? I heard Dr. David Jeremiah, senior pastor of Shadow Mountain Community Church, once say that next to Jesus, Paul was perhaps the greatest man to ever live. Some people even call him Saint Paul. Paul was a powerful teacher, preacher, missionary, and evangelist whom God used to convert literally thousands of Jews and Gentiles back in the first century.

Yet Paul said in verse 18, "I know I am rotten through and through." The New American Standard renders it this way, "For I know that nothing good dwells in me, that is, in my flesh; for the willing is present in me, but the doing of the good is not."

In verse 24 he added, "Oh, what a miserable person I am!" The King James Version reads, "Wretched man that I am!"

How about you? Would you consider yourself to be "rotten through and through" or even "wretched" like Paul?

THE REAL YOU

Let's take a short multiple choice quiz. How would you answer the following questions?

1) Apart from Christ, I am _nothing_.
   a. terrific
   b. silly
   c. mediocre
   d. nothing

2) What good can I produce on my own?
   a. It depends on how good of shape I'm in
   b. Everything I do is good—I'm self-sufficient
   c. Lots if I really try
   d. None

3) Now that I am a Christian, is my struggle with sin over?
   a. Absolutely! I don't sin anymore whatsoever.
   b. Sure it is. Why do you think I became a Christian in the first place?
   c. Maybe?
   d. Absolutely not!

We have within us a sinful nature. We were born that way. None of us, no matter how hard we try can live our lives without sin. We cannot do it. It is literally impossible. After all, 1 John 1:8 reads "If we claim to be without sin, we deceive ourselves and the truth is not in us."

Apart from Christ we are nothing. We are incapable of producing any good on our own. And just because we are Christians certainly doesn't mean that our struggle with sin is over. (By the way, I hope that you answered "d" to all of the questions above.) Paul, formerly Saul, even after a dramatic conversion experience on the road to Damascus, still struggled with the sin within him (v. 20). And like it or not, so do we.

However, because we have this sinful nature, is that an excuse for wrong living? Can we as Christians live any way we want to and just blame our "bad self" on our sinful nature? Absolutely not! That is classic Antinomian thinking. Antinomianism is a belief that existed (and still exists today) when Paul wrote this letter to the Romans. In short, it is the belief that because we are all under God's grace we can live any kind of life we desire. It is the idea that we don't need to adhere to the Law because we live by grace. Furthermore, it is a belief that the more we sin, the more God's grace abounds.

This is an absolutely ludicrous way of thinking and very far from Biblical truth. You see, as we grow spiritually and mature in Christ, we begin to understand what God wants from us and how He wants us to live. We become more and more aware of what grieves the Holy Spirit that dwells within us. We become more sensitive to that grief increasing our desire to honor Him with every aspect of our lives. Conversely, if we are not growing and maturing in Christ, we will remain oblivious to what grieves the Holy Spirit and continue to live lives that are not pleasing to our Heavenly Father.

Ephesians 4:30 reads, "Do not grieve the Holy Spirit of God." The NLT reads this way, "Do not bring sorrow to God's Holy Spirit by the way you live." In other words, we need to get a handle on our own sinfulness so that we can live our lives in obedience to God and glorify Him. In order to do that, let us take a moment and have a closer look at sin.

What is it? In the Greek, sin is related to an arrow missing the mark. On one hand that's a great word picture. But on the other hand, "missing the mark" can sound trite and inconsequential. So, perhaps in the most practical terms, sin is a deliberate disobedience to the known will of God. Sin is a revolt against the holiness and sovereign will of God. It's a condition of our mind, heart, and will coupled with the outworking of that condition in thoughts, words, and deeds that offend our Heavenly Father.

CATEGORIZING SIN

Can we categorize sin in degree of severity? Can we say that one sin isn't as severe as others? Is there a "sin scale" that we can readily use to measure our sin? No, there isn't. But, for the sake of definition, let's categorize sin in terms of external and internal. Let's think of external sins as those that are visible and conscious. For example, we would say adultery, theft, murder, abuse, addictions, etc. are external expressions of sin. We can see them. There is visual evidence of these sinful behaviors. Internal sins, on the other hand, are invisible or internal. Pride, jealousy, greed, bitterness, etc. would fall into this category.

Which ones do you struggle with more? Is it the external sins or internal sins? Which ones do most Christians struggle with more? My guess is that the majority of our struggles fall into the *internal* sins category. The internal sins are tricky. They are much harder to identify. Many times these sins deal with thoughts and emotions that are inside us. Granted, sometimes those thoughts and emotions surface and go on display for others to see (much to our chagrin). But we can't necessarily see envy, for instance. Sometimes those internal sins remain hidden and in the dark. And that is where we like to keep them. Heaven forbid anyone shine a light on our internal sinfulness and expose us for who we really are. We don't want to be found out. We don't want anyone to see the *real* us, do we? Even the best of us can appear so "saintly" on the outside, yet be so sinful on the inside.

SIN IN THE JUNGLE

On May 27, 2001, Martin and Gracia Burnham, American missionaries in the Philippines, were kidnapped by a terrorist group called the Abu Sayyaf. During a year in captivity they endured physical abuse, exhaustion, and starvation. They witnessed gunfire and bloodshed, yet managed to keep their faith in God. Gracia made it out alive—not completely unharmed, but alive. Martin, however, did not.

Reflect on the following excerpt from Gracia Burnham's book, *In The Presence of My Enemies,* which details the events of their terror in the Philippine jungle:

> "You know," Martin said to me one day, "here in the mountains I've seen hatred; I've seen bitterness; I've seen greed; I've seen covetousness; I've seen wrongdoing." I nodded my head vigorously, thinking back to incidents I had observed as well.
>
> But then he surprised me. He hadn't been talking about the Abu Sayyaf as I had assumed.
>
> "I've seen each of these things in myself. The Lord has been showing me how incredibly sinful I am." He then proceeded to go back through the list.

"Hatred? At times I have hated these guys so strongly. When we were getting cheated out of food, I'd sit and think, *Wow, I wish I had a big pot of rice, and they were the ones chained to a tree. I'd sit there and eat it all in front of them.*

"At other times, when one of them pulled out a 'personal' snack from their stash and ate it, I coveted it rather than being happy for that person."

He kept going through the list. We talked about how our hearts are wicked, and how we had rationalized that by saying we were the ones being wronged and so our feelings were only "natural."

"But Jesus said to love your enemies...do good to those who hate you...pray for those who despitefully use you," Martin continued. "He said we were to be the servants of all – and he didn't add an exception clause like, 'except for terrorists, whom you have every right to hate.'

"Let's just ask the Lord to work out some contentment in our hearts and teach us what he wants us to learn."[1]

Martin Burnham, despite this treacherous year in the jungle, admitted like the Apostle Paul that he was "rotten through and through." Martin's struggle wasn't external at all. Martin's struggle was the sinfulness deep within him that he had to deal with even as a victim of a terrorist kidnapping. His, as was Paul's, is the struggle within each of us. It is the struggle of our flesh. And unfortunately our flesh, our sinful nature, can rear its ugly head anytime, anywhere.

DAVID'S WANDERING EYES

The internal sins, if left unattended to, can quickly manifest themselves externally. If we covet enough, for example, we might commit robbery. If our hatred rises beyond a certain manageable level, it may lead to abuse or worse. The internal struggle sometimes spews forth an outward manifestation of tragic proportions. That is precisely what happened to King David in 2 Samuel 11. When David's wandering eyes landed on Bathsheba the bathing beauty, his lust, pride, and covetousness led him right into adultery and later the murder of Bathsheba's husband. However, King David did not quite see the truth about himself yet. But Nathan, a prophet of God who served King David, did. And, under the Lord's prompting, Nathan confronted David.

When Nathan exposed David for the sinful man he really was in 2 Samuel 12, David's immediate response in verse 13 was, "I have sinned against the LORD." Now, without going any further, that may seem like a very trite response on David's part. However, in Psalm 51 we have been given David's "journal entry" based on the events of the eleventh and twelfth chapters of 2 Samuel. We are privileged to see into the very heart of David in this wonderful prayer he recorded for us. David gives us the most incredible example to follow in our prayer time when we, too, have been made aware of our own sinfulness.

Read David's prayer slowly, considering his heart and the remorse and guilt he felt because of his great sin against the Lord:

> ¹Have mercy on me, O God, because of your unfailing love. Because of your great compassion, blot out the stain of my sins.
> ²Wash me clean from my guilt. Purify me from my sin.
> ³For I recognize my shameful deeds—they haunt me day and night.
> ⁴Against you, and you alone, have I sinned; I have done what is evil in your sight. You will be proved

right in what you say, and your judgment against me is just.

⁵For I was born a sinner—yes, from the moment my mother conceived me.

⁶But you desire honesty from the heart, so you can teach me to be wise in my inmost being.

⁷Purify me from my sins, and I will be clean; wash me, and I will be whiter than snow.

⁸Oh, give me back my joy again; you have broken me—now let me rejoice.

⁹Don't keep looking at my sins. Remove the stain of my guilt.

¹⁰Create in me a clean heart, O God. Renew a right spirit within me.

¹¹Do not banish me from your presence, and don't take your Holy Spirit from me.

¹²Restore to me again the joy of your salvation, and make me willing to obey you.

(Psalm 51:1-12, NLT)

What a wonderful model for us as Christians. When we come face to face with our sinfulness, what is the correct response from us? What can we learn from David's prayer?

PRAYING THROUGH OUR SINFULNESS

First, when we come before God in prayer we must recognize our shameful deeds (v. 3). In this prayer David admitted his fault, his error, and his weakness. He owned up to his own sinfulness. He did not make excuses for what he had done. Once we admit our sinfulness we tend to quickly blame it on something or someone else, don't we? We feel the need to defend ourselves so that the true burden of error does not lie with us. David did not try to explain or justify his way out. He didn't blame his sinfulness on loneliness or the stresses of being a military leader. He recognized his shameful deeds. He owned up to them. He knew what he had done and he knew it was shameful.

Second, though our sins may have had dramatic effects on others, it is ultimately against God that we have sinned (v. 4). David's sins of adultery and murder had profound effects on Bathsheba's family and on his own. He willfully disobeyed God and ultimately his actions grieved the Holy Spirit of God. His confession was to his Creator—not to his priest, best friend, or anyone else. David sinned against God and he admitted it.

Third, we should ask God to purify and wash us (vs. 2 and 7). David didn't want to be stained and blemished any more. He wanted to be clean and new and to start fresh. 1 John 1:9 reads, "If we confess our sins, He is faithful and just and will forgive us our sins and purify us from all unrighteousness." Sometimes our own sinfulness makes us so corroded and filth-covered on the inside that we literally need to be bathed in His forgiveness.

Finally, and perhaps most importantly, we should ask God to make us willing to obey Him (v. 12). It is here that confession ends and repentance begins. What's the difference? Confession is when we admit our wrongdoing. Repentance is feeling sorrowful about that wrongdoing. When we say "I'm sorry" many times we're not truly sorry for the wrong we committed. We're truly sorry we got caught! But with repentance, we are deeply and genuinely feeling guilt or remorse. We have a deep sense of shame for our sin and a firm resolve not to commit the same sin in the future. Our "I'm sorry" becomes "I'm sorry I hurt you and I will make an appropriate change." If we would walk in obedience to God in the first place, we wouldn't be in the position of asking for forgiveness in the second place.

TEAR STAINED

I believe David was very broken when he penned this prayer. If you ask me, Psalm 51 was probably a "tear stained" journal entry. He likely wept over this sin greatly and wept when he wrote out the beautiful prayer that followed.

Do we weep over our sin? I remember hearing Kay Arthur, founder of Precept Ministries International, ask that once. And my response back then was, "Uh . . . no." But, honestly, I was not walking as closely with God then as I am now.

Several years ago I was abruptly confronted with my own sinful nature as I had never been before. I was attending a class on the Fruit of the Spirit (Galatians 5:22-23). The teacher kept reiterating to us that love, joy, peace, patience, kindness, goodness, faithfulness, gentleness, and self-control were not our nature. They were the fruit that the Holy Spirit of God develops in us as we walk closely with Him. Every week she reminded us that these things were not our nature. The more she said it, the more I began to question, "If those things are *not* my nature (good person that I was), then what exactly *is* my nature?" As I prayed through that, it wasn't long until God began to reveal to me what my true nature was. Prideful. Critical. Impatient. Selfish. It was at that time in my life when I first began to weep over my sin. It was at that time that I drew ever so close to God, praying that He would transform me.

The more closely I walk with Him, the more my love grows for Him. And when I hurt those I truly love, it hurts me right back. So it is with my sinfulness and God. The more I walk in disobedience the more I know that God grieves over me. The more He grieves over me the more I hurt deep inside because of that.

"To truly weep at not having God's holiness, you must long for God's holiness. To truly weep over not possessing it, it must be attractive to you. So you see how strange this seems at first: God and His way of holiness must become your joy before you can weep over not having it. You must fall in love with a person, before estrangement really hurts."[2]

If we are not weeping over our sin—if we are not that bothered when we disobey God—I would challenge that we are not walking as closely to God as we think we are. Our desire should be to walk in obedience to God. Our hearts should be set on not grieving the Holy Spirit of God, but in glorifying Him with all of our words, deeds, thoughts, actions, and reactions.

BLINDED

We tend to think of ourselves as pretty good natured people, don't we? After all, we *are* Christians. Just the name implies our goodness. Of course all of our words, deeds, thoughts, actions, and reactions are always perfect because we *are* churchgoers. And Christians who go to church are some of the best people in this world. Right? Wrong! Emphatically wrong! Christians can be some of the most hateful, prideful, greedy, hypocritical, self-serving people around without even knowing it.

King David was a perfect example of this. He did not even realize he was prideful, lustful, and greedy. Nathan had to point this out to him (2 Samuel 12). Sometimes God uses others to open our eyes to how wretched we really are. We definitely need those other people in our lives. David definitely needed Nathan. As painful as it was to hear from Nathan that David's sin had gotten the best of him, he needed to hear it because he couldn't see it in himself.

When David was made aware of his unacceptable, sinful behavior his response was the prayer of Psalm 51. When we are made aware of our sinfulness, what's our response? How about praying similarly to David in Psalm 51?

MIRROR, MIRROR

Do you remember the story of Snow White and the Seven Dwarfs? Snow White's mother died giving birth to her. Her father, the King, took another wife who was "a beautiful woman, but proud and overbearing, and she could not bear to be surpassed in beauty by anyone."[3] The Queen had a magic mirror that she would stand in front of and say, "Mirror, mirror on the wall, who is fairest of us all?" Then the mirror would answer, "Queen, thou are the fairest of us all!" Thus the Queen was satisfied because she knew the magic mirror spoke the truth. Until one day... Upon the Queen's asking, the magic mirror responded, "Queen, thou are the fairest in this hall, but Snow White's fairer than us all." "This gave the Queen a great shock, and she became yellow and green with envy, and from that hour her heart turned against Snow White and she hated her. And envy and pride like ill weeds grew higher in her heart every day until she had no peace day or night."[4] We all know the rest of the story...

By peering into her magic mirror, the Queen discovered a cold, hard truth. She wasn't the fairest after all. The mirror revealed that she wasn't what she thought she was.

We don't have any such "magic mirrors" to gaze into and hear back from. But we do have a "spiritual mirror" that we need to frequently look into to see if we are really all we think we are—to see if there may be a hard truth we need to hear.

Several years ago, I met regularly with a small group of women (there were four of us altogether). I remember one woman bringing up Psalm 139:23-24 which reads "Search me, O God, and know my heart; test me and know my anxious thoughts. See if there is any offensive way in me, and lead me in the way everlasting." It was a passage of Scripture that she had decided to pray through for a period of time. She shared with us the importance of God bringing to her mind the things in her life that weren't pleasing to Him. She prayed this Scripture often and God began to reveal sinful things in her that were previously unknown to her. As she prayed, she (like King David) began to recognize her own shameful deeds. The New Life Bible Version of Psalm 139:23-24 reads "Look into me, O God, and know my heart. Try me and know my thoughts. See if there's any sinful way in me and lead me in the way that lasts forever." What a great prayer of the Psalmist. What a great prayer for us.

By praying this short prayer, we are peering into our "spiritual mirror" and instead saying, "Lord, Lord, Lord of all, teach me, teach me where I fall." We must come face to face with our own sinfulness. We must see it looking back at us. We must see our ugliness for what it truly is. In order to do this we need to ask ourselves some key questions: Are our thoughts, motives, and behaviors really in line with God's Word? Are we honoring and pleasing God by walking in obedience to Him?

You see, by praying this prayer we are opening ourselves up to the possibility of hearing some cold, hard truths from our Heavenly Father. This is absolutely essential if we are serious about being *fully* devoted to Jesus Christ.

Peer into your spiritual mirror. Hear what God has to say back to you. If there is indeed any offensive way in you, confess it. Use David's prayer in Psalm 51 as a model. Then choose to walk in obedience to God.

"Therefore, if anyone cleanses himself from these things, he will be a vessel for honor, sanctified, useful to the Master, prepared for every good work" (2 Timothy 2:21, NAS).

Let the Master transform you so that you can be such a vessel!

MAKING IT REAL

1. Are you acutely aware of your own sinfulness? Have you ever paused long enough to think about it?
2. Read Psalm 139:23-24 every day this week. Ask God to reveal your true nature.
3. Use David's prayer in Psalm 51 as a model for your confession this week.
4. Whom do you need to forgive this week? Whom do you need to ask forgiveness from this week? Go make it happen.

4

In Crisis? Cry Out!
(2 Chronicles 20:1-26)

"**9**-1-1, what's your emergency?" the voice on the other end of the line asked.

"Excuse me?" I replied.

"9-1-1, what's your emergency?" the voice asked again.

"Oh, that's a good one," I said, thinking my friend was trying to be funny.

"Ma'am, this is the 9-1-1 operator. Do you have an emergency?"

I didn't have an emergency. I was just trying to call a friend with a 913 area code and apparently I had inadvertently dialed 9-1-1 instead. Oops! Realizing my blunder—and quite embarrassed—I said, "No, ma'am, I don't have an emergency. I accidentally dialed the wrong number." (I never understood how one could accidentally call 9-1-1. Now I do!) I quickly hung up and carefully dialed the *right* number, told my friend the story, and both of us had a good laugh.

When we have a true emergency, we have the luxury of dialing 9-1-1. We have instant access to someone trained to handle our emergencies and walk us through solutions. And if the situation warrants, help arrives within minutes.

IMPROPER HANDLING

What about when we are in a crisis? What do we do then? How do we handle a health crisis, a financial crisis, a marriage crisis, an emotional or spiritual crisis, etc.? Many people react differently when they are in a crisis situation. Here are some different ways that people handle a crisis. See if any of these behaviors ring true with you:

- *Cover up.* You knowingly hide the crisis from the outside world. You don't let anyone know you are struggling in any way.
- *Give up.* You can't take it any more. You have no strength, no will power, no desire to overcome, so you cave in; you throw in the towel; you admit defeat.
- *Deny you have a crisis.* This is similar to covering up, but you don't want to admit you are actually in a crisis. You talk yourself into believing that "it's not that bad." When other people confront you about it, you readily change the subject.
- *Panic.* You freak out! Fear and terror strikes you in such a way that you may act or think illogically and/ or irrationally.
- *Fall apart completely.* Emotionally, mentally, physically, you simply break down. Your body displays everything your heart and soul and mind is feeling.

I ran across a humorous illustration of how Charlie Brown's friend Linus (of the cartoon "Peanuts") handles problems. One day Linus and Charlie Brown were walking along and chatting with one another. Linus said, "I don't like to face problems head on. I think the best way to solve problems is to avoid them. In fact, this is a distinct philosophy of mine. No problem is so big or so complicated that it can't be run away from!" That statement by Linus is very telling, isn't it? It reveals his true character. As a matter of fact, if you want to reveal the true character of an individual, put him or her in a crisis. If you want to know what someone is really like on the inside, watch him or her handle a crisis. Our behavior in crunch time speaks volumes, doesn't it?

THE CHARACTER OF A KING

Nestled within the pages of the Old Testament is a great story of a king whose character was revealed when he was faced with a crisis. King Jehoshaphat was king of Judah. He was one of the few good and godly kings that they had. Let's take a look:

> ¹After this, the Moabites and Ammonites with some of the Meunites came to make war on Jehoshaphat.
>
> ²Some men came and told Jehoshaphat, "A vast army is coming against you from Edom, from the other side of the Sea. It is already in Hazazon Tamar" (that is, En Gedi).
>
> ³Alarmed, Jehoshaphat resolved to inquire of the LORD, and he proclaimed a fast for all Judah. ⁴The people of Judah came together to seek help from the LORD; indeed, they came from every town in Judah to seek him.
>
> ⁵Then Jehoshaphat stood up in the assembly of Judah and Jerusalem at the temple of the LORD in the front of the new courtyard ⁶and said:
>
> "O LORD, God of our fathers, are you not the God who is in heaven? You rule over all the kingdoms of the nations. Power and might are in your

hand, and no one can withstand you. ⁷O our God, did you not drive out the inhabitants of this land before your people Israel and give it forever to the descendants of Abraham your friend? ⁸They have lived in it and have built in it a sanctuary for your Name, saying, ⁹'If calamity comes upon us, whether the sword of judgment, or plague or famine, we will stand in your presence before this temple that bears your Name and will cry out to you in our distress, and you will hear us and save us.'

¹⁰"But now here are men from Ammon, Moab and Mount Seir, whose territory you would not allow Israel to invade when they came from Egypt; so they turned away from them and did not destroy them. ¹¹See how they are repaying us by coming to drive us out of the possession you gave us as an inheritance. ¹²O our God, will you not judge them? For we have no power to face this vast army that is attacking us. We do not know what to do, but our eyes are upon you."

¹³All the men of Judah, with their wives and children and little ones, stood there before the LORD.

¹⁴Then the Spirit of the LORD came upon Jahaziel son of Zechariah, the son of Benaiah, the son of Jeiel, the son of Mattaniah, a Levite and descendant of Asaph, as he stood in the assembly.

¹⁵He said: "Listen, King Jehoshaphat and all who live in Judah and Jerusalem! This is what the LORD says to you: 'Do not be afraid or discouraged because of this vast army. For the battle is not yours, but God's. ¹⁶Tomorrow march down against them. They will be climbing up by the Pass of Ziz, and you will find them at the end of the gorge in the Desert of Jeruel. ¹⁷You will not have to fight this battle. Take up your positions; stand firm and see the deliverance

the LORD will give you, O Judah and Jerusalem. Do not be afraid; do not be discouraged. Go out to face them tomorrow, and the LORD will be with you.' "

¹⁸Jehoshaphat bowed with his face to the ground, and all the people of Judah and Jerusalem fell down in worship before the LORD. ¹⁹Then some Levites from the Kohathites and Korahites stood up and praised the LORD, the God of Israel, with very loud voice.

²⁰Early in the morning they left for the Desert of Tekoa. As they set out, Jehoshaphat stood and said, "Listen to me, Judah and people of Jerusalem! Have faith in the LORD your God and you will be upheld; have faith in his prophets and you will be successful." ²¹After consulting the people, Jehoshaphat appointed men to sing to the LORD and to praise him for the splendor of his holiness as they went out at the head of the army, saying:

"Give thanks to the LORD,

for his love endures forever."

²²As they began to sing and praise, the LORD set ambushes against the men of Ammon and Moab and Mount Seir who were invading Judah, and they were defeated. ²³The men of Ammon and Moab rose up against the men from Mount Seir to destroy and annihilate them. After they finished slaughtering the men from Seir, they helped to destroy one another.

²⁴When the men of Judah came to the place that overlooks the desert and looked toward the vast army, they saw only dead bodies lying on the ground; no one had escaped. ²⁵So Jehoshaphat and his men went to carry off their plunder, and they found among them a great amount of equipment and clothing and also articles of value—more than they could take away. There was so much plunder that it took three days

to collect it. ²⁶On the fourth day they assembled in
the Valley of Beracah, where they praised the LORD.
This is why it is called the Valley of Beracah to this
day.

(2 Chronicles 20:1-26)

This passage of Scripture is absolutely loaded with both
life lessons and prayer lessons. This passage of Scripture is
one that I have referred people to when they are just struggling with life. It teaches us how to act, how to react, how to
pray, and how to listen. If you need to, go back and read the
passage again . . . slowly. Read to understand. Put yourself
into the story.

First of all, let us recall the crisis at hand. "The Moabites
and Ammonites with some of the Meunites came to make
war on Jehoshaphat" (v. 1). Now, I don't know about you,
but if my neighborhood all of a sudden declared war on my
family I think I would freak out just a little. And my guess
is that King Jehoshaphat did too. The NIV calls his reaction
"alarmed." The Message calls it "shaken." The NAS reads
he "was afraid." Would any of these words describe you in
the same situation?

LESSONS ON LIFE

As I stated earlier this passage is loaded with life lessons
as well as prayer lessons. What does King Jehoshaphat do in
reaction to the news he heard?

Life Lesson #1: Jehoshaphat goes first to God (v. 3). He
"turned his attention to seek the Lord" (NAS). How many
times do *we* try to fix our problem first? How often is our
first reaction to pick up the phone and call a friend, spouse,
church member, etc.? It is almost as if God is sometimes our
last resort. I cannot tell you how many conversations I have
been in or been a part of in which people share a struggle

they are facing. And the question is raised to them "Have you prayed about that?" Dead silence. Deer in the headlights. Then comes their true confession . . . "No, I haven't!" Because what we try to do is wrap our brains around the crisis first. We try to understand it. We try to retrace our steps, figure out why it happened. If we could figure out the cause, maybe we could figure out the solution. Then we explain it to someone else in hopes that they can help us understand it and figure it out. Then we read up on the issue in order to get educated so that we can again try to come up with a solution. Then . . . finally . . . when we've exhausted all our other possibilities, we go to the One who is greater than us *and* our crisis, and we ask for help. Jehoshaphat, however, went straight to the Source first. What a great model for us when we are faced with any crisis.

After the king sought the Lord for guidance he made an amazing proclamation.

Life Lesson #2: Jehoshaphat orders a fast (v. 3). What is a fast? A fast is an abstinence from something for a set period of time and for a set purpose. Fasting was an expected discipline in both the Old and New Testament days. Jesus said, "When you fast..." (Matthew 6:16). He didn't say "If you ever get around to fasting..." It was expected. Moses fasted (Exodus 34:28). David fasted (Psalm 35:13). Jesus, Himself, fasted (Luke 4:1-2).

We fast, first and foremost, to glorify God. We fast because we are waiting on a specific answer from God. Quite honestly, I believe fasting is a lost discipline among Christians today. Most of us have either never or seldom participated in a fast. "Fasting must forever center on God. It must be God-initiated and God ordained."[1] Our one and only intention is to glorify God. "Fasting can bring breakthrough in the spiritual realm that will never happen in any other way. It is a means of God's grace and blessing that should not be neglected any longer."[2] Fasting can be a powerful spiritual discipline. When we fast and pray, we humbly deny something of the flesh in order to glorify God. We take our eyes off the things of this world and instead focus on God. When we fast and pray, we open ourselves up to transforming power of the Holy Spirit. And transformation is exactly what happened to King Jehoshaphat and the people of Judah.

Life Lesson #3: People gathered together (v. 4). I don't know how people go through the difficult circumstances of life without being part of a church family. When Hurricane Katrina hit New Orleans in August of 2005 many people had nowhere to go, so they left the state. Some of them left for good. I remember thinking, "Don't you have a church home, a church family to help you?" The concept of being without people to come along side them during a most difficult time was absolutely foreign to me. I cannot even fathom the thought.

We have a family in our church whose home was destroyed by a tornado in May of 2003. Both Tom and Amy testify that they would not have made it through that year-long process of rebuilding without their church family, support, prayers, meals, clothing, babysitting, etc.

Another family in our church was told their three-year old son had cancer. Instead of covering up this crisis or denying it or hiding it, they brought it before the church. The church walked with them, prayed with them, called them, visited them, stayed with them, wept with them, laughed with them, and provided for them through surgery and many months of chemotherapy. And the church is still rejoicing and praising God with them years later as Scott remains cancer-free. That is the body of Christ! And that is the privilege we have to be a part of it!

These families experienced first hand, as did King Jehoshaphat and the people of Judah, the body of Christ. We need each other! We are not called to be Lone Rangers in the faith. We are commanded to do life together! Time and again, Scripture confirms this fact. We are called to:

- Pray for each other (James 5:16, NIV)
- Bear with each other (Colossians 3:13, NIV)
- Encourage each other (1 Thessalonians 4:18, NIV)
- Build each other up (1 Thessalonians 5:11, NIV)
- Be concerned about each other (Hebrews 13:1, CEV)
- Help each other have a strong faith (Romans 14:19, CEV)
- Love each other (John 15:17, 1 Peter 4:8, NIV)
- Forgive each other (Ephesians 4:32, NIV)
- Be at peace with each other (Mark 9:50, NIV)

And this is only a partial list! "Each other" is one of the most precious gifts the Father has given us—one that we too often take for granted. The people of Judah understood the "each other factor." And they gathered together to seek the Lord.

LESSONS ON PRAYER

When the people had gathered together—when they gave their "each other-ness" to King Jehoshaphat at the temple—he speaks directly from his heart to God. Our first instructional moment begins with Jehoshaphat's first words.

Prayer Lesson #1: Jehoshaphat acknowledges God (v. 6). How many times do we dive right into our quiet times of prayer and Bible study and do not even acknowledge the presence of God? All too frequently, during our daily quiet times or even at our worship services, we come into God's presence flippantly, not really sensitive of how awesome He truly is. The first thing Jehoshaphat said in his prayer was "O LORD, God of our ancestors, you alone are the God who is in heaven. You are ruler of all the kingdoms of the earth. You are powerful and mighty; no one can stand against you!" (2 Chronicles 20:6, NLT). Basically he was saying, "I recognize that YOU are God. YOU are awesome. YOU are powerful. YOU are mighty. And nothing compares to YOU!" Unlike us, he didn't immediately state his need and sole purpose in praying. He didn't instantly focus on what was wrong or bad in his life. He first focused his attention on the One who is right and good! Many prayers throughout Scripture begin with giving praise and honor and glory to God. Those doing the praying recognize first and foremost to Whom they are praying. We, too, should initially approach God's throne offering Him the awe and reverence He deserves!

Prayer Lesson #2: Jehoshaphat cries out to God (v. 9). Out of curiosity I searched for the words "cried out to the Lord" in the Old Testament. I found that phrase used twenty-six times in the New Living Translation Bible. Interestingly, twenty-five out of the twenty-six times when people cried out to the Lord, the Lord answered. More specifically He showed, He gave, He sent, He granted, He provided, etc. The only time God did not directly answer His people when they cried out to Him was in Exodus 14:10b-11. The NLT reads "The people began to panic, and they cried out to the LORD for help. Then they turned against Moses and complained..." After crying out to God, the Israelites disparaged Moses for bringing them out in the desert to die. Their "crying out to God" was essentially just whining and complaining to Moses. And God didn't act based on their "crying out." As a matter of fact, He questioned it by saying to Moses, "Why are you crying out to me? Tell the people to get moving!" (Exodus 14:15, NLT).

Jehoshaphat, however, sincerely cried out to God. In his prayer, he poured out his heart before God. Lamentations 2:19 reads "Pour out your heart like water in the presence of the Lord." In your prayer time, don't be in "drip mode," only allowing a few droplets of your heart to trickle out. Open the faucet of prayer. Don't be afraid or ashamed to let it gush out. Be like David who said in Psalm 57:2, "I will cry to God Most High, to God who accomplishes all things for me" (NAS). And also in Psalm 18:6, "But in my distress I cried out to the LORD; yes, I prayed to my God for help. He heard me from his sanctuary; my cry reached his ears" (NLT). We will look at how to specifically cry out to God in prayer at the end of this chapter.

Prayer Lesson #3: Jehoshaphat admits his dependence (v. 12). Hear once again what Jehoshaphat prayed: "For we have no power to face this vast army that is attacking us. We do not know what to do, but our eyes are upon you." Where do we look in times of crisis? As I stated earlier, I fear we look everywhere but to God. Psalm 105:4 reads, "Look to the LORD and his strength; seek his face always." Do we always look to the Lord? Do we always seek His face?

I agree with Dr. David Jeremiah who once said, "Prayer is our declaration of *de*pendence!" King Jehoshaphat was as honest as he could be in this part of his prayer. He didn't pretend to have the answers. He didn't pretend to have the solutions. He didn't pretend that his ability or his knowledge to handle this situation was any greater than it truly was. But he knew where to go for the answers. He knew where to place his trust. More specifically, he understood in Whom to place his trust. He knew not to depend on himself, but to depend fully on the Almighty God.

LISTENING TO WISE COUNSEL

What happened in the few verses following the conclusion of King Jehoshaphat's prayer in verse 12 should not be disregarded. It furnishes us with one more profound instruction.

Life Lesson #4: Jehoshaphat listens to wise counsel (v. 14-17). Sometimes we don't seek wise counsel. Sometimes when we seek it, we ignore it. And sometimes when we seek wise counsel we don't receive it. The net effect is the same—we miss out. God has given spiritual gifts to His children. To some He has given the gift of discernment. To others He has given the gift of knowledge or wisdom. Still to others He has given prophecy or faith. Why don't we listen to those people whom God has gifted? We need those people in our lives. Sometimes our own perspectives or viewpoints are skewed or out of line. Sometimes we need an alternate opinion because our view is obscured by our own involvement in the situation. King Jehoshaphat was given a gift in the person of Jahaziel. Jahaziel came directly to the king full of godly wisdom.

What was this godly wisdom he gave King Jehoshaphat (and essentially Israel)? First he said profoundly in verse 15, "Do not be afraid . . . the battle is not yours but the Lord's." A vast army was coming against Israel and Jahaziel told them to not be afraid. (Yeah, right!) Furthermore, he added that the battle was not theirs, but God's. If our battles are indeed God's battles, then why do we feel like we are the only ones fighting them?

Second, Jahaziel added in verse 17 (in the New Living Translation), "Take your positions; then stand still and watch." I don't know about you, but when there is a battle going on and I find myself in the middle of it, the last thing I want to do is stand still and watch.

Both of these pieces of godly wisdom, however, were not only good but golden. The best and biggest and hardest thing we can do in the midst of crisis is get out of the way and let God be God! Deuteronomy 1:29-30 reads, "Do not be terrified; do not be afraid of them. The LORD your God, who is going before you, will fight for you, as he did for you in Egypt, before your very eyes..." God is going before us in our every battle; in every footstep of our crisis, God is going before us. What a promise! The Almighty God is fighting for us. Therefore, Psalm 46:10 makes all the more sense then — "Be still, and know that I am God." What matters most is not that we know these Biblical truths, but how we respond to them.

RESPONDING TO WISDOM

How did King Jehoshaphat respond? He "bowed with his face to the ground...in worship" (v. 18). Did he *accept* this wisdom and insight given him by Jahaziel? Or did he *embrace* it? What's the difference? Let me give an example. For instance, we can *accept* the policy change at our work place that says we can wear shorts to work during the summer months. We don't particularly like the new policy. Perhaps we might think it's quite unprofessional. But we can accept it without causing any waves with management. Or we can embrace the policy change. We can believe that the change is positive, act on it, and incorporate change by wearing shorts ourselves.

Regarding Jehoshaphat, if he would have merely accepted the wisdom, he would have simply agreed to it or relented to it because he had a certain level of understanding of it. But instead I believe he embraced it. He not only adopted the godly wisdom, but he incorporated it fully. He immediately acted upon the wisdom he was given. He bowed down in worship to God because he believed every word of it wholeheartedly. By believing, incorporating, and acting on the godly wisdom given to him, he fully embraced it. Jehoshaphat didn't waver. He didn't flinch. He had solid hope, conviction, and confidence that the Lord would be with him, that he would not have to fight the battle, and that the Lord would truly deliver him. What a lesson in unshakeable faith!

67

What was the result of this unshakeable faith? A massive slaughter. Not by Jehoshaphat and his men, but by the enemies themselves. They destroyed each other! There was no enemy for Jehoshaphat and his men to fight. And after three days of plunder, "they gathered . . . and praised and thanked the Lord there" (v. 26, NLT).

CRUCIALS IN CRYING OUT

When Jehoshaphat's men cried out to God in time of crisis, the result was victory! Three things are crucial if we are to cry out to God in our own time of crisis.

First, be specific. As you are praying through your crisis, ask God for specific answers. Let me give you an example. Suppose you are struggling financially and you ask me to help you. I would love to help you but I don't know exactly what you need. Do I need to write you a check or give you cash immediately? Would it help you if I went to the grocery store and bought you two weeks of groceries to see you through until your next pay day? Should I help you find employment? Maybe I should sit down with you today and help you budget your money for the next month and hold you accountable to that. You see, I could help you in a variety of ways, but when you describe your wants and needs specifically, I know better what you want and need in that particular situation.

You may be thinking to yourself, "Why be specific in my prayers? Doesn't God already know what I need?" Absolutely. He's all-knowing and all-powerful. He is fully in tune with our needs. But I believe God wants us to be specific when we pray. How can He answer if all we say is "help me!" or "make this situation better!"? God may choose to answer us in these types of prayers, but we may not recognize His help when He sends it. Similarly, He may do something for us to make the situation better, but we remain oblivious because we weren't specific. But, when we ask God in specific ways to answer our prayers, then it is easier to thank and praise Him when those specific prayers are answered.

What if, in our effort to be specific, we ask for the wrong thing? Well, I believe God has a way of either changing our request or changing us in the process. I don't believe He sends wrong answers in response to our wrong requests. He lovingly spares us those things and gently points us in the right direction.

Second, when we cry out to God, be audible. Get someplace where it is just you and God; somewhere that you can have a conversation with God and be heard. I don't mean to indicate that God cannot or will not hear us if we pray silently. But there is something about praying out loud that allows our minds and hearts to stay focused on what we are saying and to Whom we are saying it. I do better in my own personal prayer time when I can hear myself. I get less distracted. I actually feel like I am having a conversation with the Almighty God who is sitting right there beside me.

King David did the same thing. He said in Psalm 142:1 "I cry aloud with my voice to the LORD; I make supplication with my voice to the LORD" (NAS). In other words, he prayed out loud. We have much to learn from this man who God refers to as a "man after My own heart" (Acts 13:22).

Finally, when we cry out to God, don't hold back! God wants to hear from us. God desires to bless us. He knows our hearts anyway. Who better to communicate our hurting hearts to than our Creator? When we let it all out in prayer, not holding anything back, we sometimes reveal to ourselves the depth of our struggle. Not only that, but we empty ourselves of the pain, hurt, and conflict within and lay it all at the feet of a God who cares about every detail of our lives—even the ugly stuff.

By crying out to God, will He always change our circumstances? No, not unless it is His will to do so. There are many things He will not change. But that is because He has a higher and better purpose. Oh, to be able to see that higher and better purpose. But if we could, there would be little or no need for faith.

How will you handle your next crisis? Cover it up? Or cry out? Recall one last time the words of King Jehoshaphat, claiming the words of his ancestors, "If calamity comes upon us...we will stand in your presence...and will cry out to you in our distress, and you will hear us and save us" (2 Chronicles 20:9).

MAKING IT REAL

1. Revisit the question "How do you handle crisis?" Give yourself an honest assessment. After this chapter's lessons how are you encouraged to handle crisis differently?
2. Which one of King Jehoshaphat's life lessons do you need to adopt for yourself? And how will you make that happen?
3. Which one of King Jehoshaphat's prayer lessons do you need to adopt for yourself? And how will you make that happen?
4. In your prayer time this week, cry out to God about some difficult situation(s) in your life and watch God go to work! If you keep a journal or diary, document those situations, your prayers, and God's answers. Doing that can reveal the faithfulness of our great God.

5

Passion → Prayer → Pursuit
(Nehemiah 1:1-11; 2:1-5)

Romeo and Juliet is arguably one of the most powerful displays of passion ever written. In it, the Montagues and the Capulets hated one another passionately. Yet Romeo Montague and Juliet Capulet were deeply in love. Their passion for each other, despite the feuding of their families, led to premature death for them both. Romeo, believing his beloved Juliet was dead, drank poison to put an end to his grief. Juliet, who faked her own death initially, upon hearing of Romeo's suicide, took her beloved's dagger and slay herself. It is a tragic story of love, and war, and passion.

Can you even relate to that story? Think about it for a moment. One man—so passionate about love, that when he couldn't have it, he took his own life. One woman—so zealous for love, that when she couldn't have it, she took her own life. What are you *that* passionate about? What kinds of things stir in you so deeply that you would risk your reputation, your savings, your job, even your life to get your deepest heart's desire?

THE PASSION OF THE CUPBEARER

Let us take a look at one such man in the Old Testament named Nehemiah. Nehemiah was a Jew, who lived in Persia, and served as cupbearer to King Artaxerxes. In order to understand who Nehemiah was, we need a brief history lesson. About 586 B.C., the Babylonians (the ultimate "bad guys") wiped out Jerusalem. They burned the temple and tore down the city walls. The Jews were then sent out of Jerusalem and scattered throughout the land. Around 539 B.C., the Persians defeated the Babylonians. In the years following, some of the previously scattered Jewish exiles returned to Jerusalem. Then, around 445 B.C., Nehemiah received some news.

> [1]The words of Nehemiah son of Hacaliah: In the month of Kislev in the twentieth year, while I was in the citadel of Susa, [2]Hanani, one of my brothers, came from Judah with some other men, and I questioned them about the Jewish remnant that survived the exile, and also about Jerusalem. [3]They said to me, "Those who survived the exile and are back in the province are in great trouble and disgrace. The wall of Jerusalem is broken down, and its gates have been burned with fire." [4]When I heard these things, I sat down and wept. For some days I mourned and fasted and prayed before the God of heaven.
>
> (Nehemiah 1:1-4)

Imagine one of your relatives visiting you and informing you that those you knew and loved from across the country were in bad shape and having all kinds of trouble. Your heart would sink. It would break with worry and concern. You might even struggle over what to do next.

Nehemiah, who was the cupbearer to the king and of Jewish heritage, took an opportunity to do some catching up with his visiting brother Hanani. Upon the arrival of Hanani and some other men from Judah, Nehemiah "questioned them about the Jewish remnant." After all, they were his people, his heritage, and his ancestors. He cared, he was concerned, so he initiated an inquiry. He could have chosen to insulate himself, but he didn't. He genuinely wanted to know. And his passion for his people was immediately revealed when he was informed about their plight.

THE RISK OF GETTING INVOLVED

Are we that genuine? Do we genuinely want to know how someone is doing in the midst of their possible struggles? Sometimes it's easier for us to stay at arm's length in situations like these. Unaware. Unattached. Less knowledge equals less pain. If we don't look too closely at the lives of our friends and, sometimes our family, then we don't feel the responsibility to act.

But Nehemiah inquired because he genuinely wanted to know "about the Jewish remnant that survived the exile and also about Jerusalem." He cared tremendously. And he was willing to embrace whatever answer he received from his question. "Those...in the province are in great trouble and disgrace." Not the answer he was hoping for. His people were in bad shape. "The wall...is broken down and its gates burned." Even worse! His people were left exposed. No city walls or gates meant no protection.

At this point Nehemiah's spirit was broken; his heart was crushed. Verse 4 reads, "When I heard these things, I sat down and wept. For some days I mourned and fasted and prayed before the God of heaven." Mourned. Fasted. Prayed. What kinds of things stir in you so deeply that you would mourn, fast, and pray? Nehemiah's passion was once again revealed.

THE STIRRING WITHIN

Have you ever heard of the term "holy discontent"? I heard Bill Hybels, pastor at Willowcreek Church, use this term once. According to Mr. Hybels, holy discontent is a term that is used to describe the one thing that grabs you by the throat and won't let you go. It is something that moves you to the core. It's something that so unsettles you it prompts a definite, measurable response.

Take Moses and the maltreatment of his people in Egypt, for example. He was so appalled by the abuse of his fellow Hebrews that he did something about it. Or take David and Goliath. David was similarly disgusted by Goliath's "bully-like" treatment of his fellow Jews and it caused him to take action. You see, something powerful stirred deep within both Moses and David . . . so much so that they could not sit idly by. It didn't matter how small or insignificant or ill-equipped Moses and David thought they were, the stirring in them was so strong they couldn't neglect it any longer. And God used them to accomplish something extraordinary. Their "holy discontent" caused them to take action on God's behalf.

Nehemiah's passion for his people led him immediately to prayer. What better response is there when our hearts are crushed and our spirits are broken?

[5]Then I said:

"O LORD, God of heaven, the great and awesome God, who keeps his covenant of love with those who love him and obey his commands, [6]let your ear be attentive and your eyes open to hear the prayer your servant is praying before you day and night for your servants, the people of Israel. I confess the sins we Israelites, including myself and my father's house, have committed against you. [7]We have acted very wickedly toward you. We have not obeyed the commands, decrees and laws you gave your servant Moses.

⁸"Remember the instruction you gave your servant Moses, saying, 'If you are unfaithful, I will scatter you among the nations, ⁹but if you return to me and obey my commands, then even if your exiled people are at the farthest horizon, I will gather them from there and bring them to the place I have chosen as a dwelling for my Name.'

¹⁰"They are your servants and your people, whom you redeemed by your great strength and your mighty hand. ¹¹O Lord, let your ear be attentive to the prayer of this your servant and to the prayer of your servants who delight in revering your name. Give your servant success today by granting him favor in the presence of this man."

I was cupbearer to the king.

(Nehemiah 1:5-11)

THE CHARACTER OF THE CUPBEARER

In these seven verses, Nehemiah revealed several things about his own character. We see his conviction, his confession, his confidence, and his commitment.

Nehemiah began his prayer displaying his deep conviction about God's character. He acknowledged God right away. He did not begin his prayer with whining. He began it with worship! Several of the prayers we have looked at began precisely this same way. Men and women of the Bible, despite varying circumstances and different eras, acknowledged God's greatness, His majesty, and His sovereignty. "O Lord, God of heaven, the great and awesome God..." (Nehemiah 1:5). Nehemiah's heart and mind were immediately centered upon the greatness of God, not the greatness of his pain.

From his conviction about God's character, he moved into a confession of sins. There was urgency—"...let your ear be attentive and your eyes open to hear..." (Nehemiah 1:6). It's almost as if Nehemiah was saying, "God, I hurt to the core. So right here and right now, Lord, hear me!"

There was intensity—"...praying before you day and night..." (1:6). This was not just a one time prayer. He prayed day and night. He was persistent. He was consistent. Recall Paul's words in 1 Thessalonians 5:17 "Pray continually." He continually turned his passion into prayer.

There was honesty—"I confess the sins *we* Israelites, including myself and my father's house, have committed against you. *We* have acted very wickedly toward you. *We* have not obeyed the commands, decrees and laws you gave your servant Moses" (Nehemiah 1:6-7, emphasis mine). It's interesting to me that Nehemiah did not lay the blame on his Jewish ancestors. He did not tell God how sinful *they* had been. Instead, he identified with them. Even though he was not part of that particular group of Jews, he knew that he was equally as sinful. Where there is sin, there must also be contrition.

After a confession of sins, Nehemiah declared his confidence in God's promises. The promise in verse 8 had already been fulfilled. The unfaithful had already been scattered. But the promise in verse 9 was yet to be fulfilled. Nehemiah placed his confidence in the promise God made to Moses that if his people (even the unfaithful, exiled ones) returned to God and obeyed His commands, He would gather them together again. Nehemiah put into practice what the writer of Hebrews encouraged us all to do. "Let us hold unswervingly to the hope we profess, for he who promised is faithful" (Hebrews 10:23). Nehemiah was confident that God would indeed deliver what He had promised. I've heard it said that there are some 7,000 promises in the Bible. The better we know the Word of God, the better we will be able to pray with confidence in His promises. Oh, that we would share this same confidence in this same God that Nehemiah worshiped and served!

THE COMMITMENT OF THE CUPBEARER

After declaring his confidence in God's promises, Nehemiah expressed his commitment to get involved. "Give your servant success today by granting him favor in the presence of this man" (Nehemiah 1:11). He prayed with a heart that was ready to do something. He prayed poised to take action. He had resolved to make his commitment to this cause official by making his appeal to the king that he served.

The true measure of our concern is not based on how many times we inquire about a particular situation. The true measure of our concern is based on our willingness to get involved. Nehemiah's concern was genuine and he was ready to embrace a commitment to get involved.

Nehemiah's passion for his people led him immediately to prayer. His prayer led him to pursuit.

[1]In the month of Nisan in the twentieth year of King Artaxerxes, when wine was brought for him, I took the wine and gave it to the king. I had not been sad in his presence before; [2]so the king asked me, "Why does your face look so sad when you are not ill? This can be nothing but sadness of heart."

I was very much afraid, [3]but I said to the king, "May the king live forever! Why should my face not look sad when the city where my fathers are buried lies in ruins, and its gates have been destroyed by fire?"

[4]The king said to me, "What is it you want?"

Then I prayed to the God of heaven, [5]and I answered the king, "If it pleases the king and if your servant has found favor in his sight, let him send me to the city in Judah where my fathers are buried so that I can rebuild it."

(Nehemiah 2:1-5)

Nehemiah first heard of the plight of the Jewish remnant "in the month of Kislev" (Nehemiah 1:1). Here in Chapter 2 "In the month of Nisan..." indicates that this was four months after Nehemiah's initial prayer. Four months had gone by before Nehemiah went to King Artaxerxes with a huge request. What did he do in those four months? Lose his passion? Lose sight of his goal? Forget all about this deep stirring that had occurred within him earlier? Not hardly! My guess is that God was making all the necessary preparations in Nehemiah, in King Artaxerxes, and in all others who were essential to His plan.

In the four months that elapsed, I would bet that Nehemiah undoubtedly bathed this situation in prayer day after day. He probably prayed for the right opportunity to approach the king and the right words to say. He may have prayed for God to open a door . . . and for the courage to step through it. He waited for his God-ordained opportunity to arrive. Then it did!

King Artaxerxes noticed the sadness in his servant Nehemiah's face and confronted him about it. (Aha! The door had opened.) God presented Nehemiah an opportunity in which to share his pain and passion with the king. Nehemiah recognized this God-given moment and stepped up to the plate.

But before he swung for the bleachers, he threw up what I call a bullet prayer—those quick prayers that are shot straight up to heaven in the heat in the moment. When King Artaxerxes asked Nehemiah what it was that he wanted, Nehemiah "prayed to the God of heaven" then answered the king. He had bathed this situation in prayer for four months. Now he shot up one last prayer before making his request.

Bullet prayers. I pray them all the time. As a matter of fact, I prayed one last week while I was out walking in my neighborhood. A lady I didn't know stopped me and asked me if I'd help her set her yard waste by the side of the road for the next day's pickup. She went on to share with me how her husband had died unexpectedly a few days prior and she had never taken care of the yard waste until that day. My heart sank! I quickly threw up a bullet prayer and prayed that God would give me words to say to her. And He did. I helped her with the bags and limbs while I asked her some questions and listened to her tell her story. I ended our conversation with a simple statement that I would pray for her. God heard and honored that bullet prayer. He heard and honored Nehemiah's too.

In verse 5, Nehemiah laid his request before the King. He wanted to go to Jerusalem and help rebuild the wall. He wanted to pursue the passion that he had bathed in prayer. So, he did!

It only took 52 days to rebuild the wall, but Nehemiah laid the foundation with four months of prayer before that. How often do too many good works fail because we hurry them? I've seen it all too often. In people's lives, in church's lives—the great ideas and plans fail, because God's people fail to pray fervently before putting the ideas and plans into motion.

Several people (including Martin Luther, Saint Augustine, Ignatius of Loyola) are given credit for the statement "Pray as if everything depends on God, then work as if everything depends on you." I'm not sure who first said it, but Nehemiah certainly lived it out. Then he pursued his passion with great fervor, confident in God's faithfulness!

As I think about the passion → prayer → pursuit succession, I believe there are three different scenarios that can happen to each one of us when prompted with a particular stirring within us.

First, there's the "Passion → Wither" scenario. This is when something stirs within us; it peaks our interest and maybe even presses our passion button. But as quickly as it arises, it fades then withers away. Never prayed about. Never acted upon.

Second, there's the "Passion → Prayer → Wither" scenario. This is when something stirs within us so much so that we even pray about it for a while. But we never put any hands or feet to that prayer, so it too eventually fades then withers away. This is where I find myself a lot of times. God places something or someone in my life that gets my attention. It arouses a passion inside me. I even spend some time praying about it (maybe half-heartedly) to see what will happen next. But eventually the spark that was there initially dies out and grows cold. Sometimes that is God's way of closing the door and moving me elsewhere. But sometimes I wonder if I actually missed out on an opportunity He put in my path. And sometimes I regret not pursuing it.

And last, there's the "Passion → Prayer → Pursuit → WOW!" scenario. This is when something stirs within us, we pray about it (maybe for months or years), then instead of sitting idly by we take action. Recall the words of James, "What good is it, dear brothers and sisters, if you say you have faith but *don't show it by your actions?*" (James 2:14, NLT, emphasis mine). We pursue . . . we commit . . . and WOW! We *get* to be a part of glorifying God! We *get* to be a part of advancing His Kingdom! Can I say it again? WOW! When we as devoted Christ-followers are obediently walking the path that God has marked out for us, it doesn't get any better than that! God plants the seeds within us. We water those seeds with prayer. We do the work necessary to nurture and grow the seed into a plant. Then we get to delight in the fruit that it produces.

Is there an area in your life where you need to move your passion to prayer? Maybe you have a passion and have been praying about that. Is it now time to step up the pursuit? You might be waiting on God, but God just might be waiting on you to act in order to do something incredible in you and through you. Can you even imagine?

"Now to him who is able to do immeasurably more than all we ask or imagine, according to his power that is at work within us, to him be glory in the church and in Christ Jesus throughout all generations, for ever and ever! Amen" (Ephesians 3:20-21).

MAKING IT REAL

1. What is your "holy discontent"? Consider bathing that in prayer for an extended period of time. Be open to embrace the prompting of the Holy Spirit.
2. Incorporate some "bullet prayers" into your every day life this week and watch God go to work. Be prepared for Him to honor those, and then praise Him BIG TIME for it!
3. In Nehemiah's prayer we saw his conviction, his confession, his confidence, and his commitment. Which one of these do you need to work on in your own time of prayer?
4. Read and study the rest of Nehemiah as part of your quiet time this week.

6

Fleece Or Faith?
(Judges 6:36-40)

Have you ever seen one of those "Magic 8 Balls"? It's a black ball (a little bigger than a grapefruit perhaps) that fits in your hand. You ask a question, concentrate, shake it up, and up through a little screen comes the answer to your question. It's a great way to get the answers to life's toughest questions. Why struggle through something and wait forever for an answer when you can solve all your problems immediately by using the Magic 8 Ball?

Here, let me demonstrate. I will ask a question, meditate on the 8 ball, shake it and tell you its response.

ME: "Will the Kansas City Chiefs make it to the playoffs this year?" (I'm shaking the 8 ball.)

8 BALL: "As I see it YES!"

Cool! I love this thing. I bet you wish you had one too, right? Let me try another question.

ME: "Should I fix meatloaf for dinner?" (Shaking...)

8 BALL: "Very doubtful!"

Well, my kids will appreciate the magical yet persuasive response of the 8 ball on that one. They will forever put their hope and trust in this thing if it keeps delivering these promising results. But let me ask one more question. This time, I'll be serious. I will ask a question that I truly would love to have answered.

ME: "Will this book be published?" (Shaking... concentrating...)

8 BALL: "Reply hazy, try again!"

I don't care for that response...

ME: "Will this book ever be published? (Shaking harder...)

8 BALL: "Outlook not so good!"

Not cool! I don't like this thing any more! I want to keep shaking it until I get a better answer. Then I will know my true destiny, my fate, God's will for my life. (Yeah, right!)

DISCOVERING GOD'S WILL

Isn't it is interesting how we go about finding answers to life's difficult questions? Isn't it fascinating how we some-times attempt to determine God's will or direction in our lives?

How do we *know* where God is leading us? How can we be sure of God's will or His direction for our lives? It is a common struggle with Christians when considering career choices, marriage, parenting, tithing, etc. And we have several ways in which we go about seeking God's will. Some are good; some are not so good.

Some go for the "random finger method." This is similar to the "Magic 8 Ball." In this method, you ask the question that is greatly burdening you, randomly open your Bible, and with eyes closed plop down your finger. And in some magical way, the verse that your finger landed on is your "divine answer." Burden lifted! Problem solved! Not hardly! The problem with this method is you could literally spend hours randomly poking and prodding your way through Scripture searching again and again for a favorable response, let alone one that even made any sense relevant to your question.

There are others that go for the "miraculous event method." This would be like Moses and the burning bush, or Saul on the road to Damascus. We seek God's will by waiting (or hunting) for those mind-blowing, phenomenal, unbelievable events. We determine that if God really wants us to change jobs, for instance, then He's going to send some kind of incredible sign. Then, and only then, will we make a move believing that our "sign" is indeed of God. I don't doubt that God can still work that way today. But personally, I haven't seen a bush smoldering nor have I been blinded by a heavenly light while on my routine walks in our neighborhood. And if this is the method we are using, we might be waiting for a long time for our answer.

Another method of determining God's direction for our lives is the "striking coincidence method." This is the bargaining method with God in which we say something like, "God, if you want me to increase my tithe this year, then make the telephone ring within the next two minutes." And for the next two minutes, we hold our breath and stare at the phone...waiting...wondering. If the phone does indeed ring, we think God must have spoken directly to us and we must in fact increase our tithe. If the phone does not ring, however, we conclude that God must not be interested in any more money from us. The hitch here is that we fail to recognize that the telephone ringing (or not ringing) could actually be a coincidence. The telephone ringing is a common occurrence. So are red lights, black cars, clouds in the sky, or whatever other test you ask God to pass.

Yet another technique is the "open door/closed door" approach. This one is actually tricky. We might say, "Lord, if You want me to go to college at _____, then please open the door for me." Or, "God, if You do not want me to accept this job transfer, then please close the door for me." While I truly believe that God does open and close doors for us, we must proceed with caution here. We should make sure that *we* are not pushing the doors open ourselves. Similarly, we mustn't mistake a door closed by God with a door slammed by us. We might slam God's open door shut because He is calling us to something that might be a stretch for us. The real question in this method is *who* is doing the opening and closing.

The "still small voice method" is one that is widely used by Christians today. Some would describe it as a peaceful answer deep within them, a quiet prompting inside their souls. For those who have experienced this as determining God's direction or will, they might say it was indescribable, or powerful, or amazingly peaceful. But there are others who maybe have not experienced this feeling who would raise a legitimate question: how do you determine whose voice is speaking? How do you know that it's not the voice of your own desire, or the voice of the Deceiver whispering untruths to you? Good questions. Tough answers.

GIDEON'S METHOD

We will look specifically at how to pray and how prayer assists us in determining God's direction for our lives later in the chapter. For now I want to focus our attention on a man named Gideon.

As we enter the life of Gideon in Judges 6, we are immediately informed that "Again the Israelites did evil in the eyes of the LORD, and for seven years he gave them into the hands of the Midianites" (Judges 6:1). (The Israelites had this cycle of good living, then bad living. God stepped in, they straightened up for a while, then the cycle began again.) So, God decided to use the Midianites to punish the Israelites. The Midianites were a hostile and oppressive people. They came at harvest time every year and totally wiped out the

Israelites' crops and livestock. "Midian so impoverished the Israelites that they cried out to the LORD for help" (Judges 6:6). Guess what God did? He gave the Israelites a stern correcting! We tend to think spoiled or unruly children are the only ones who need rebuking these days. But that couldn't be farther from the truth. Proverbs 3:11-12 reads, "My child, don't reject the LORD'S discipline, and don't be upset when he corrects you. For the LORD corrects those he loves, just as a father corrects a child in whom he delights" (NLT). What a wonderful reminder of the perspective we all should have when God corrects us.

God, however, doesn't just rebuke the Israelites and angrily walk away. No! Gracious God that He is, He devised a plan to rescue them from their troubles. He approached a modest, unassuming guy named Gideon and said, "The LORD is with you, mighty warrior . . . Go in the strength you have and save Israel out of Midian's hand. Am I not sending you?" (Judges 6:12 and 14). Now Gideon was anything but a mighty warrior. As a matter of fact, he was more like the "runt of the litter" (Judges 6:15, MSG). But God insisted and persisted and promised Gideon that he would indeed strike down all the Midianites.

Gideon was now in a bit of a dilemma. He needed to be sure of God's will for him. He needed a surefire method of determining God's direction. He opted for the "miraculous event method." He went to prepare a sacrifice to God. He brought it before the Lord, and "With the tip of the staff that was in his hand, the angel of the LORD touched the meat and the unleavened bread. Fire flared from the rock, consuming the meat and the bread. And the angel of the LORD disappeared" (Judges 6:21). Whoa! I don't know about you, but that would definitely convince me.

Meanwhile, the Midianites and the Amalekites had joined forces and were positioning themselves to attack Gideon's people. But Gideon, even after his "miraculous event," still lacked confidence in God's leading. So, he prayed. But this prayer is much different than the ones we have looked at previously. As a matter of fact, nothing about it remotely resembles a prayer. It's just a conversation with God. But wait a second . . . isn't that what prayer is? Isn't it communication with God? Isn't it speaking to and hearing from our Heavenly Father? Absolutely! So here is Gideon's prayer:

> [36]Gideon said to God, "If you will save Israel by my hand as you have promised— [37]look, I will place a wool fleece on the threshing floor. If there is dew only on the fleece and all the ground is dry, then I will know that you will save Israel by my hand, as you said." [38]And that is what happened. Gideon rose early the next day; he squeezed the fleece and wrung out the dew—a bowlful of water.
>
> [39]Then Gideon said to God, "Do not be angry with me. Let me make just one more request. Allow me one more test with the fleece. This time make the fleece dry and the ground covered with dew." [40]That night God did so. Only the fleece was dry; all the ground was covered with dew.
>
> (Judges 6:36-40)

How many of us want to be 100% sure before we step out and do something new, different, uncomfortable, etc.? As we try to determine God's will for our lives in a particular situation, how sure do we have to be before we step out in faith? 100% sure? 75% sure? If I'm being honest, when it comes to the big stuff, I want God's will to be crystal clear. I want 100% clarity. I don't want to worry about the missing 10-25%. I want to know beyond a shadow of a doubt. But if we think about that—if all our actions were based on God's 100% guarantee—then do we leave any room for faith? Would we have any need for faith at all?

Gideon was going for the 100%. So he put God to the test. "Show me a sign!" he said. He put out a fleece of wool and said, "If You make this wool wet and make the ground dry, then I'll know You are going to come through on what You said." God was tested. God passed. Gideon doubted. Gideon tested God again. "This time make the wool dry and the ground wet." God was tested. God passed. Gideon was finally convinced. By testing God, he had received the proof he needed.

PUT GOD TO THE TEST

Is it really okay to put God to the test? Should we? Should we follow Gideon's example and "put out a fleece" to determine God's will or direction for our lives? Is it okay to ask God for signs of His approval — either the approval of our plans or the approval of a decision that we think might be His will?

Scripturally speaking we could build cases both for and against putting God to the test. First, let's build a case in favor of putting God to the test.

Matthew 14:25-29: This is the story of Jesus walking on water out to the disciples in the boat. They were terrified; they thought Jesus was a ghost. But Peter said, "Lord if it's you…tell me to come to you on the water." And Jesus said, "Come." Peter basically said to God, "If it's really You, then prove it!" And prove it, He did!

Malachi 3:10-12: God reprimanded the Israelites by telling them that they were robbing Him in their tithes and offerings. They were cheating Him by only giving a small portion, not truly a tithe. So He said to them, "Bring the whole tithe into the storehouse, that there may be food in my house. Test me in this…and see if I will not throw open the floodgates of heaven and pour out so much blessing that you will not have room enough for it." Wow! God Himself said "test Me." If He said it, then shouldn't we do it?

John 20:24-29: The disciples had seen the risen Christ and most of them believed. However, one doubted. Thomas. "Unless I see the nail marks in his hands and put my finger where the nails were, and put my hand into his side, I will not believe it." Thomas wanted proof. One week later, Jesus appeared to Thomas and gave him the "hands-on" evidence he desired. "Put your finger here; see my hands. Reach out your hand and put it into my side. Stop doubting and believe." Thomas was immediately convinced.

Psalm 78:18-24: The Psalmist, speaking about the Israelites' forty years of wandering in the desert, said "They willfully put God to the test by demanding the food they craved" (v. 18). The Israelites—hungry, yet stubborn and rebellious—mocked God. They even spoke against God, whining and complaining, crying "He can strike a rock so water gushes out, but he can't give his people bread and meat," (v. 20, NLT). God heard and was furious with the people of Israel. However, "he rained down manna for the people to eat, he gave them the grain of heaven" (v. 24). Victory for the Israelites!

Now, if we stop here, it looks as though we have established a pretty solid case in favor of putting God to the test when we doubt or when we have a need. But now let's focus our attention on passages in God's Word that strongly oppose putting God to the test.

DON'T PUT GOD TO THE TEST

John 20:24-29: Yes, this is the same passage listed in the previous section in support of testing God. But note what Jesus said to Thomas (and to the rest of those present) after Thomas received his "proof." In verse 29 Jesus told him, "... blessed are those who have not seen and yet have believed."

The Amplified Bible reads this way: "Blessed and happy and to be envied are those who have never seen Me and yet have believed and adhered to and trusted and relied on Me." If we can believe God without putting Him to the test, we are blessed, happy, and to be envied.

Matthew 16:1-4: The Pharisees and Sadducees (both religious leaders of sorts) demanded that Jesus show them a miraculous sign. They wanted their proof just like Thomas. What they got instead was a blasting from Jesus: "A wicked and adulterous generation looks for a miraculous sign, but none will be given it..." Jesus called the "proof-pursuers" wicked, adulterous, evil (NAS), and morally unfaithful (AMP). Yikes! Maybe this testing God thing isn't such a good idea after all.

2 Corinthians 5:7: Very simply put, Paul said "We live by faith, not by sight." We live for, love, serve, and are willing to die for a God that we've never seen. We are confident, as Paul explained in the fifth chapter of 2 Corinthians, of spending an eternity in the presence of our Lord, not because we've already seen Him, but because we take God at His Word. This is faith! When we keep demanding facts and evidence and proof, there is no room for faith! If, however, we hold fast to the faith we possess, we won't need to put God to any test.

Deuteronomy 6:16: Moses reported everything that God told him to report to the Israelites. This entire chapter is a call for wholehearted commitment from the Israelites to the Almighty God. He said to them loud and clear, "Do not test the LORD your God as you did when you complained at Massah." Wow! If God said *not* to test Him, then we should not test Him!

So, do we or don't we put God to the test? Are there risks involved when we put God to the test? Are there risks involved if we don't? For some of us it's a tough question. For others, it's an easy answer. We'll draw some conclusions about testing God later in the chapter. I'll admit I have also wrestled with this question: "Should I or should I not test God?"

MY OWN TESTING

Now I must confess to you that I have actually "put God to the test" twice in my life. The first time was when I was a young teenager. I was sitting on my bed pondering life. And I don't really know what possessed me to do this, but I said to God, "God if You are real, send a purple car down the road to pass by our house." Okay, I realize this prayer was just ridiculous. A purple car? Are you kidding? We lived in the country where not many cars went down our road. But I asked God to send a purple car. Hey, I figured God could pull it off if He wanted. Well, needless to say, He wasn't up to the challenge that day (probably because He was rolling His eyes and shaking His head at me). I soon quickly forgot about the test I gave Him.

The second time I "put God to the test" was about three years ago. A dear friend was struggling through a deep depression; struggling with the will to live. One particular night, she had hit rock bottom—tired of struggling, weary of the depression, the battle had taken its toll mentally, physically, emotionally, and spiritually. She was ready to put an end to her life. I remember going to my bedroom, hitting my knees, and with my fists clenched and tears rolling down my face I cried out, "God, if You really are who You say You are, then prove it! Intervene right now in the life of my friend!" And gracious, loving, kind, and merciful God that He is, He did intervene. Not only that, but He has walked her through an amazing emotional and spiritual healing.

DRAWING CONCLUSIONS ABOUT TESTING GOD

Let me ask you a question. When we put God to the test, what is it we are really seeking? Are we seeking a sign from God? Or are we seeking God Himself? I would challenge that when we seek a sign from God, we are not truly seeking God. We are merely putting our faith and trust in the "sign" rather than trusting God. Matthew 6:33 reads, "But seek first His kingdom and His righteousness, and all these things will be added to you" (NAS). We are to seek the Blesser, not the blessings. Seek His face, not His hands. Seek the Sovereign God, not His signs.

Whether or not you are in favor of "testing God"—in Gideon's case his "testing'" was in the form of "putting out fleeces"—there are three conclusions we can draw. *First, putting out the fleece was a sign of unbelief.* Putting God to the test is an indication of our weak faith. In Gideon's case, he already had two promises and a sign. He already knew what God was calling him to do. But his unbelief caused him to question that calling, so he tested God by putting out the fleeces. Where was his faith?

Upon rebuking the wind and the raging waters at sea, Jesus asked His disciples, "Where is your faith?" (Luke 8:25). Jesus asks me this same question quite often. And I, like the disciples in Luke 17:5, say back to Him, "Increase my faith!" And I also respond like the father of the boy with the evil spirit who said to Jesus, "I do believe; help me overcome my unbelief!" (Mark 9:24). God and I have these conversations frequently. What I have discovered is that God continues to act despite my lack of faith. And I don't think He'll stop acting. He wants me to fully grasp His love and faithfulness. He wants us all to trust Him completely. I don't know about you, but I want to trust Him the first time. I want to have that kind of unshakeable faith.

Second, putting God to the test is like putting God in a box. When we put conditions on our prayers, we are essentially putting conditions on God. We say to Him, "Here are my parameters, my boundaries, and my requirements I want You to meet. If You do, then I'll totally trust You." When we put God to the test we expect Him to fit the mold we give Him. God is much bigger than our list of so-called requirements. God is much bigger than the boxes we give Him to fit into. And maybe, just maybe, God wants to deliver more to us than the contents of our "boxes."

Finally, putting God to the test is really putting ourselves to the test. When we put God to the test we ultimately are the ones who are thus tested. In many instances we have to act on what we pray. Recall in Matthew 14 when Jesus walked on water out to the disciples in the boat. Remember Peter's "test"? He said, "Lord, if it's you . . . tell me to come to you on the water" (Matthew 14:28). Jesus, meeting Peter's challenge, said, "Come." He challenged Peter right back. Peter was put to the test. He had to get out of the boat and actually set his foot on the water. Scary!

I wonder what Peter thought as he stepped out of the boat. "This is nuts!" "I can't believe I'm doing this!" But for a brief moment, after he "tested" God—after he was "tested" by God—he actually walked on water. But that meant he had to act. Peter, himself, had to pass a test.

Recall God's words in Malachi 3: "bring the whole tithe into the storehouse . . . Test me in this . . . and see if I will not throw open the floodgates of heaven and pour out so much blessing that you will not have room enough for it" (Malachi 3:10). If we are going to "test" God in the area of our tithe, He is going to "test" us right back. We are the ones who actually have to write out the check for more than what we normally might do, and drop it in the offering plate as it passes by. We have to act.

And let's not forget Gideon. In the same way, after Gideon "tested" God, God challenged Gideon right back. Remember, the Midianites and the Amalekites had joined forces and were positioning themselves to attack Gideon's people. Gideon gathered his troops, all thirty-two thousand of them, and prepared for battle. But God told Gideon that his army was too big—that if the Israelites won this battle they would brag on their own efforts. So God made Gideon go through a "weeding out" process with his army. Gideon watched as his army of thirty-two thousand dwindled down to a mere three hundred. God said to Gideon, "I'm going to rescue Israel by helping you and your army of three hundred defeat the Midianites" (Judges 7:7, CEV). I would have freaked out, but Gideon didn't flinch. He passed God's test. He had to act on what he prayed.

PUTTING PRAYER TO THE TEST

So maybe we should change the question we considered previously from "Is it fair to test God?" to "Have I fairly tested prayer?" You see, when faced with a weighty decision, sometimes we *think* about it for long periods of time. Sometimes we ask other folks and listen to their advice. There is nothing wrong with thinking and listening. But too often, that's all we do. Or we do much more thinking and listening to others than we do praying about the decision we need to make. Maybe that's simply because thinking and listening are easier than praying.

How should we pray when we need to discern God's will or direction in our lives? How do we fairly test prayer?

Pray with a willingness to be obedient. How many times do you go to God in prayer with your mind already made up? "God, there's no way we can afford to increase our tithe this year, but we'll pray about it because the pastor said to." With a mindset like that we will very likely miss out on something extraordinary God has for us.

We should echo the words of King David in Psalm 51:12 "Restore to me again the joy of your salvation, and make me willing to obey you" (NLT). Lord, make us willing to obey You! When we honestly seek God's direction or will for our lives it is absolutely imperative that we pray with a willing and obedient spirit to go where He leads.

Give prayer a fighting chance. Our prayer lives sometime resemble a lousy football team. After running three plays that make no advances up the field, they're faced with fourth and long. So, they punt. Similarly, we pray for God to point us in the right direction, we don't make any progress, then we punt. We have to give prayer a fighting chance. Nehemiah prayed for four months before he set out for Jerusalem. Four months may seem like a long time to a lot of folks. Paul encourages us to "pray continually" (1 Thessalonians 5:17). God's answer might be waiting on our fourth down response. Punt or go for it? Punt or keep praying?

Pray in faith. "But when he asks, he must believe and not doubt, because he who doubts is like a wave of the sea, blown and tossed by the wind" (James 1:6). Sometimes we struggle to believe that God really does care about our problems. Sometimes we question whether or not He really is listening. Or we might even hold the attitude that He's too busy fixing the "bigger" problems of the world. Occasionally we might even think He can't handle our problems. When we pray without doubt and hesitation, God faithfully answers if it aligns with His will. That's a promise. "If you believe, you will receive whatever you ask for in prayer" (Matthew 21:22).

If you're currently struggling with faith or belief (or lack thereof), then let me reiterate what I said previously in this chapter. God and I frequently have conversations in which I say (like the disciples in Luke 17:5), "Increase my faith!"

The Message translation of that same verse reads "The apostles came up and said to the Master, 'Give us more faith.'" In your struggle, go to the Master and ask Him to increase your faith.

Finally, when we are honestly seeking an answer from God we need to pray and listen. Have you ever encountered one of those "conversation hogs"? You know the type— the ones who talk and talk and talk and don't let you get a word in edgewise. They might ask you a question but then don't let you answer because they answer it for you. It's totally one-sided and you walk away wondering who their next "victim" might be. All of us are actually quite good at being "conversation hogs" in our prayers. We talk and talk and talk. We don't let God get a word in edgewise. We ask Him questions and answer them for Him. I wonder if He is constantly trying to remind us of Psalm 46:10 "Be still, and know that I am God..." God can communicate to us in our prayers if we would just listen to what He is trying to say.

ESSENTIALS

Prayer is absolutely essential when we are trying to figure out where God is leading us, when we are seeking answers to life's difficult questions, and when we are faced with tough questions. I believe in the power of prayer. I believe in the God to Whom I am praying. But prayer is not the only avenue of hearing from God.

Be a disciple of the Word! You've probably heard those "Bible thumpers" who keep insisting that your answers are in the Word. Well, I hate to tell you this, but they're right. God absolutely does provide answers in His Word. He continually reminds me to be a woman of the Word, and amazingly He speaks loud and clear through it. I am blown away by the fact that when I ask God, He directs me to a specific passage of Scripture to answer my specific questions. He brings to my mind over and over again a passage, a story, a character in His Word that directly relates to the issues I'm dealing with. Deep within my spirit He guides me to what He wants to show me. As I grow more in the knowledge of God's Word, I can also direct other people to passages that deal specifically with what they're going through. That's pretty cool. And so is our God!

Seek wise counsel! Seek out people in your church, small group, Bible study, etc. with the spiritual gift of discernment, or knowledge, or wisdom. Surround yourselves with two or three of these folks and let them help you think objectively, pray with you and for you, and let them use their God given gifts to bless and encourage you as you seek answers.

And finally pray like you mean it! Believe that God will indeed answer you. Watch Him go to work. And don't forget to share those victories with those who have walked with you along the way.

MAKING IT REAL

1. Read through Judges 6 – 8 this week to see the rest of Gideon's story. Immerse yourself in the Word of God. Soak up all that He has for you in these chapters.
2. Think about your own prayers. How do you pray— with fleeces or with faith? Has it always been this way for you or have your past experiences shaped how you pray?
3. When you pray for God's direction or will for your life, which one of these four components do you need to improve on—praying with a willingness to be obedient, giving prayer a fighting chance, praying in faith, or praying and listening?
4. If you are currently struggling with some deep questions of God's will for your life, make a commitment right now to do two things: faithfully spend time

in the Word allowing God to direct you to what He wants you to read, and call a couple of folks today who can journey with you.

7

When Life's Not Fair
(Habakkuk 3:1-19)

When I was eleven years old my parents gave my brothers and me a motorcycle for Christmas—a little Kawasaki 90 that we rode all over our 40 acres in the country. I loved it! I loved riding through our woods, our pastures, our corn or soy bean fields—popping wheelies, going fast, splashing through the mud. What freedom . . . what energy . . . what excitement!

Soon a boy moved in about a half mile from us. He was a year younger than me. He and his dad lived alone. His parents had divorced. He had a much older sister as I recall; she was already on her own. So, it was just Jimmy and his dad . . . and Jimmy's motorcycle. This was all too exciting!

Together, we rode recklessly (and illegally, I might add) through every field and on every country road around us. Yes, we wrecked a few times. But we got up, shook the dust off, bandaged the wounds, and went right back out for another wild ride. (I'm not sure my parents ever realized this of course . . . but they do now!) Yes, Jimmy and I had an absolute blast riding incessantly on our motorcycles.

Well, time passed. We grew up. I went to college in Oklahoma. Jimmy joined the military. While on leave he decided to come home. He'd gotten a "real" motorcycle by then, and was legally driving it on the streets. But, Jimmy never made it home. He lost control of his motorcycle and died instantly. Tragic! A young life taken from this world. An only son taken from his father. Life didn't seem fair.

It doesn't seem fair for our dear friends in Ohio either. They are a godly couple, nearing their 40's, who have struggled for a number of years to have a child. They have tried fertility drugs and shots and have been to several different doctors looking for help. They have spent a great deal of time and money and have shed many tears holding onto their hope that God would provide.

As I consider their situation, I think, "They'd make great parents. They would raise their kids in the church. This couple would set before their kids a model of what it means to walk daily with the Lord. They are kind and caring and considerate and would pour themselves out for their children."

Just a few months ago they made the painful decision to give up trying to have their own baby. "It must not be God's will for us," they said. Now they've turned their thoughts, hearts, and prayers toward adoption.

Meanwhile, everywhere we look there are children who are born to people who do not treasure them. What an injustice—or at least to many of us it appears to be an injustice. And we can't help but think to ourselves sometimes that life just doesn't seem fair.

We are frequently faced with the age-old question: Why do *bad* things happen to *good* people? Or the opposite: Why do *good* things happen to *bad* people? We do not have to look very far to see it, do we? Turn on the news. Pick up the newspaper. Or maybe you *are* the "good people" and "bad things" are happening to you.

OUR VOICE THROUGH HABAKKUK

There was a man in Scripture who struggled with these same questions. His name was Habakkuk. There really isn't much known about him. He was a prophet. Most prophets in the Bible brought God's words to God's people. Most of them did it without much finesse. It was mostly an "in your face" method. And more often than not their message was to remind people to pay attention to what God had to say.

However, Habakkuk was different. Instead of Habakkuk bringing God's words to God's people, he brought the peoples' words to God. Although the book of Habakkuk is estimated to have been written around 623 B.C., the theme of it strikes a chord with us today. At that time, and at the present, Habakkuk gave voice to the disappointments, frustrations, and confusion God's people were experiencing. We can identify with those same disappointments, frustrations, and confusion today. And interestingly enough, unlike other Old Testament prophets, Habakkuk boldly insisted that God pay attention to His people!

Habakkuk began like most of us do when things aren't quite going our way . . . he complained:

²How long, O LORD, must I call for help? But you do not listen! "Violence!" I cry, but you do not come to save. ³Must I forever see this sin and misery all around me? Wherever I look, I see destruction and violence. I am surrounded by people who love to argue and fight. ⁴The law has become paralyzed and useless, and there is no justice given in the courts. The wicked far outnumber the righteous, and justice is perverted with bribes and trickery.

(Habakkuk 1:2-4, NLT)

Sounds like a complaint to me. Is that okay? Is it really okay to complain to God?

COMPLAINING OR HONESTY?

John Ortberg, pastor at Menlo Park Presbyterian Church, in his book *God Is Closer Than You Think*, dedicates three pages to "the gift of complaining." Read what he has to say about complaining to the Lord:

"When we are passionately honest with God, when we are not indulging in self-pity or martyrdom but are genuinely opening ourselves up to God, when we complain in hope that God can still be trusted—then we are asking God to create the kind of condition in our heart that will make resting in his presence possible again. And God will come. But he may come in unexpected ways."[1] Complaining in hope that God can still be trusted is essential. It shifts our focus from "poor me" and "I hate what I'm going through" to "This situation in my life really stinks, God, but I know You are in control." When we have the assurance of God's sovereignty in the midst of life's unfairness, it allows us to rest in His presence. What a wonderful perspective to have when things do not appear to be fair. What a wonderful attitude to have toward our own life's injustices.

Habakkuk was certainly "passionately honest" with God. Injustice was everywhere . . . and Habakkuk told God all about it (as if God were not aware). If we thought much about it, we could really get rolling on the injustices that we see today: child pornography, the rising cost of health care, lavish lifestyles for some compared to severe poverty and starvation for others, corporate downsizing, abortion, and many more. There are injustices all around us. And some of us have been first-hand victims of these injustices. "It just isn't fair!" we cry.

VERBAL COMPLAINT, VERBAL RESPONSE

Habakkuk looked and saw "sin and misery" all around him much like we do. And he got verbal about it. In return, God answered. Wouldn't we all love that? To voice our concerns and complaints straight to God and have Him answer immediately? Habakkuk actually had that experience.

God replied to Habakkuk, "Look at the nations and be amazed! Watch and be astounded at what I will do! For I am doing something in your own day, something you wouldn't believe even if someone told you about it" (Habakkuk 1:5, NLT). If we were to stop there, we would be inclined to think that God had heard Habakkuk's cry and was now going to get busy fixing all of the injustices that he complained about. Not so! As a matter of fact, God actually poured a little salt in Habakkuk's open wound. God went on to tell Habakkuk that He was going to take the Babylonians (the "bad" guys) and have them come and teach the Israelites (the "good" guys) a lesson. He was going to allow the villainous Babylonians to "punish and correct" the Israelites. As if things weren't bad enough already!

WATCH AND LEARN

Watch and learn! How hard is that? God basically said to Habakkuk, "sit back...watch and learn. I am going to work!" How hard is it to sit back ... watch ... and learn? Personally, I don't care for that method. I would prefer that God tell me immediately what it is that I'm supposed to learn and then I will straighten up and be done with it. I don't want to have to go through a long and painful learning process. I want to be good enough, smart enough, willing enough, and obedient enough to learn the lesson instantly. But unfortunately I don't learn that way. And God knows I don't learn that way. So He frequently says, "Beth, sit back...watch...and learn.

I am going to work!" That sounds delightful, but in reality, it's quite difficult.

Habakkuk, being told to "watch and learn," and being told that the "bad guys" were coming to put the hammer on him and his "good guys," complained once again to God—this time with a bit of challenging sarcasm. God's answer to Habakkuk's complaint seemed so utterly ridiculous and illogical that Habakkuk (in verses 12-17) essentially lashed back, "The Babylonians? Are You serious? You are choosing the Babylonians to come in and discipline us for our sinfulness? Are You sure You know what you are doing? I don't think that is such a good idea. That plan of Yours makes no sense to me. How long will this so-called discipline take anyway?"

Completely and utterly ridiculous! Ludicrous! Irrational! Unreasonable! That's what God's answer to Habakkuk felt like to him. How do we handle it when God's answers seem absurd? We sometimes question whether or not it was truly God who was answering. We begin "negotiating." We begin looking at other options. And like Habakkuk, we complain.

But God patiently endured Habakkuk's complaints. Nearly the entire second chapter is God's second response. He assured Habakkuk that what He said would eventually happen. He basically blasted the evil doers (the proud, the greedy, the thieves, the corrupt, etc.) of Habakkuk's time. He reminded Habakkuk that those evil doers would eventually be punished. Justice would eventually be served! Soon "good things" would stop happening to "bad people."

At the end of God's response came His powerful exclamation point to Habakkuk: "But the LORD is in his holy Temple. Let all the earth be silent before him" (Habakkuk 2:20, NLT). God is God. We're not. He is on the throne. We aren't. He reigns. We don't.

FROM PROTESTING TO PRAYING

Habakkuk went from protesting in the first two chapters to praying in the third. I do believe his complaints were indeed a form of prayer . . . after all isn't prayer a conversation with God? But notice the difference in Habakkuk's conversation with God as you read a portion of it here:

> ²I have heard all about you, LORD, and I am filled with awe by the amazing things you have done. In this time of our deep need, begin again to help us, as you did in years gone by. Show us your power to save us. And in your anger, remember your mercy.
> ¹⁶I trembled inside when I heard all this; my lips quivered with fear. My legs gave way beneath me, and I shook in terror. I will wait quietly for the coming day when disaster will strike the people who invade us. ¹⁷Even though the fig trees have no blossoms, and there are no grapes on the vine; even though the olive crop fails, and the fields lie empty and barren; even though the flocks die in the fields, and the cattle barns are empty, ¹⁸yet I will rejoice in the LORD! I will be joyful in the God of my salvation. ¹⁹The Sovereign LORD is my strength! He will make me as surefooted as a deer and bring me safely over the mountains.
>
> (Habakkuk 3:2, 16-19, NLT)

Habakkuk's powerful prayer contains four essentials for us when we feel like life isn't fair. In our own times of injustice, Habakkuk's position, his plea, his poverty, and his pressing on demonstrate how we are to respond.

First, note Habakkuk's position. Here is another example of a person in prayer who is completely humbled before God. He was "filled with awe by the amazing things" God had

107

done. Filled with awe. If you close your eyes for a moment and step back from your current situation, will you not be truly awed by God's power, love, faithfulness, grace, mercy, provision, protection, etc. that has been displayed in your life? When Habakkuk stopped to think about it, he was truly blown away by what God had accomplished in his past. His attention was redirected to the character of God rather than the circumstances around him. The impact of this redirection led him to fear the Lord.

Next, note his plea. After Habakkuk acknowledged that God was indeed God, he put forth his plea. "We desperately need You, Lord," he said. How many times have we prayed something similar? Habakkuk continued, "Right here and right now, help us, show us Your power, and remember Your mercy!" Recall that the Israelites had a track record of being "good" for a while, then "bad" for a while, then back to "good." It was an endless cycle. In reality, they needed some serious discipline. Habakkuk knew it. He knew that things were bad and according to God they were going to get worse before they got better. That's not necessarily the encouragement we long to hear. But sometimes things do get worse before getting better. God longs to leave His fingerprints on every facet of our frustrating situations, even when they get worse. He desperately wants to get our attention so that we eventually will put our weak hand in His strong hand and let Him lead.

If we look carefully in verse 16, we see a shred of faith. Habakkuk prayed, "I will wait quietly for the coming day when disaster will strike the people who invade us." It was true—good things were happening to bad people, and bad things were happening to good people. But holding on to God's promise that the ones doing the punishing would eventually be punished was a triumph of faith for Habakkuk. Eventually the wrongs would be righted. And ultimately God was (and still is) in charge of it all.

Third, in his prayer, Habakkuk admitted his poverty. He did not sugar coat anything. He was gut-level honest in his thoughts, feelings, perceptions, and emotions. Sometimes that is where we need to start. We need to stop pretending that we have it all together. We need to admit the bleakness of our circumstances. We need to confess them to God, but to others as well. How can others pray for us if they think we're fine all the time? Habakkuk's situation was bleak and he admitted it.

"Though the fig tree does not bud and there are no grapes on the vines, though the olive crop fails and the fields produce no food, though there are no sheep in the pen and no cattle in the stalls..." (Habakkuk 3:17). It would appear that everything in Habakkuk's life stunk. Destitution. Hardship. Adversity. Impoverishment. Misery. Despair. Injustice. This was the state of affairs some two thousand six hundred years ago. Unfortunately, it is still the state of affairs for many today.

Habakkuk, however, pressed on. Hear his words. Read them out loud: "...yet I will rejoice in the Lord!" (v. 18). Amazing, isn't it? In the midst of all of life's injustices and hardships, Habakkuk chose to be joyful in the God of his salvation. What a powerful choice that was! He determined to have the Lord be his strength. He chose to live out that shred of faith that he professed in verse 16. Faith isn't faith if it is just spoken. Faith becomes true faith when it is acted out. God said, "The righteous will live by their faith" (Habakkuk 2:4, NLT). *Live!* Not speak about or brag about or read about or any of those things. But *live* by their faith.

What does "living by faith" get us? Answers to that question may vary anywhere from ulcers to the ultimate God experience. Living by faith certainly isn't easy. And sometimes we do not even know what living by faith looks like, do we? "What is faith? It is the confident assurance that what we hope for is going to happen. It is the evidence of things we cannot yet see" (Hebrews 11:1, NLT). And we know that by faith "the men of old gained approval" (v. 2, NAS). If you are struggling with your own faith, receive some assurance by reading Hebrews 11. It is sometimes referred to as the "Hall of Faith." It documents the saints of Scripture who have walked by faith and done incredible things.

Habakkuk's statement of trust and faith came in the last two verses of his prayer. "God will see me through all of the mountains that stand in my way!" he said. Friends, that is a faith that presses on! Anytime we say "God will _____ _____" (fill in the blank: provide, protect, see us through, make clear, etc.), that is an incredible profession of faith in our powerful God. Press on!

THE JOURNEY OF COMPLAINT TO COMMITMENT

Habakkuk's journey in this book went from complaint to compliance to commitment. He began the book by complaining to God. Then he decided to comply with God's will. But he ended the book by committing to rejoice in the God of his salvation.

His attitude is similar to that of Job. Recall that Job was a good man who had a great family, great wealth, and great health. Then Job lost literally everything. However, he said, "But He knows the way that I take; When He has tested me, I shall come forth as gold" (Job 23:10, NKJV). What an assurance! God knows exactly what we are going through. He has a purpose for that. And when He has tested us, we will come forth as gold. Job did. And by faith, we can too!

Had Job and Habakkuk been around to read the New Testament book of James, they would have been the first to testify to its powerful truth: "Blessed is the man who perseveres under trial, because when he has stood the test, he will receive the crown of life that God has promised to those who love him" (James 1:12).

Habakkuk, Job, you, and I all experience trials of one kind or another. All of us could at one time say "Life is not fair!" But if we press on like Habakkuk, if we pray through like Habakkuk, we will "come forth as gold" and "receive the crown of life."

God can still be trusted today! We can rest in His presence! God is at work! Habakkuk, submitting to these truths, made a life changing choice. Make the choice today to be "joyful in the God of your salvation"—even when life's not fair!

MAKING IT REAL

1. What in your life would you complain about to God right now?
2. Listen for God's response to you. Be patient. Be still. And listen.
3. Think of some amazing things God has done for you—how He has provided for you, protected you, blessed you, etc. Write those down somewhere. Sit back and be filled with awe at how great our God is.
4. What does being "joyful in the God of your salvation" look like to you? How would you describe that? Make a choice beginning right now to indeed be "joyful in the God of your salvation!"

8

Time To Pinch-Hit
(Colossians 1:9-12)

pinch-hit (pĭnch'hĭt')
intr.v. **pinch-·hit, pinch-·hit·ting, pinch-·hits**

1. *Baseball.* To bat in place of another player scheduled to bat, especially when a hit is badly needed.
2. *Informal.* To substitute for another in a time of need.

Pinch-hitters. They are called upon in a baseball game to go to bat for someone else who is scheduled to hit. They have no warning. No preparation time. They just step up as called and as needed. They are not the famous ones. Nor the wealthy ones. They are not the ones you'll see on the cover of *Sports Illustrated*. But they are the reliable ones. The ones you can go to in a "pinch."

in·ter·cede (ĭn'tər-sēd')
intr.v. **in·ter·ced·ed, in·ter·ced·ing, in·ter·cedes**

1. To plead with somebody on behalf of somebody else.

2. To intervene between groups or individuals with intent to reconcile differences.

Intercessors. They are called upon to pray on behalf of someone in need. They have no warning. No preparation time. They just step up as needed. They are not famous. Nor wealthy. You won't see them on the cover of "Church Illustrated." But they are reliable. The ones you can go to in a "pinch."

Both pinch-hitting and interceding are methods of intervention. Both pinch-hitters and intercessors step in at crucial moments to alter what is happening or might happen.

In Scripture, we see example after example of people intervening to change a set of circumstances. These people "went to bat" for someone else. They were "pinch-hitters" when a hit was badly needed. They pleaded in prayer on behalf of another. They were intercessors.

King Jeroboam asked "the man of God" to pray that his shriveled hand would be restored (1 Kings 13:6). Hezekiah prayed for those who were ceremonially unclean, saying "May the LORD, who is good, pardon everyone who sets his heart on seeking God..." (2 Chronicles 30:18-19). Job prayed for his three friends who were basically wretched to him when he lost his health, wealth, and his family (Job 42:10). Samuel prayed for the whole house of Israel after they had confessed that they had not lived wholeheartedly for the Lord. "Then Samuel said, 'Assemble all Israel at Mizpah and I will intercede with the LORD for you'" (1 Samuel 7:5).

Samuel, Job, Hezekiah, Moses, Paul, even Jesus Himself interceded for others. They prayed for friends, acquaintances, and strangers alike. They intervened on behalf of other people in order to change their circumstances in some way. In many instances a "hit" was badly needed. So the intercessors got busy.

A SPORTS PERSPECTIVE

When I was in college I took a course called Sports Officiating. In it, we learned every rule of football, basketball, and baseball. We practically memorized the rule books for these various sports and had to log several hours of observation for each sport. As part of our grade, we even took the formal tests to become high school officials of each sport. Because I grew up playing sports the class was relatively easy for me. I played organized sports all the way from third grade through college. Basketball was my first love. But I also played volleyball, softball, and yes, even flag football. As I said, the class was pretty easy for me because I grew up with a sports mentality. But I will admit that learning the rules of football wasn't as easy as I thought it would be. I knew the basics: offense, defense, punt, pass, run, kick, a few positions, and point scoring. But I had no idea how complicated football was. I guarantee I know more about football than the average stay-at-home mom.

For those of you who know nothing about sports, let me give you a very brief lesson. First, there's the offense. The offense is generally the team with the ball. They are on the attack. The offense is in constant pursuit of points and ultimately in pursuit of victory. If the offense would work harder, scoring points along the way, the defense wouldn't have to work as hard when it's "crunch" time.

What is the defense? The defense guards against the attack by the opposing offense. The defense's job is to stop the pursuit of the offense. They resist the attack. In most sports the defense cannot score points. When it's "crunch" time, and their team is losing, they hunker down, give it all they've got, and rally to defend against the impending score or victory by their opponent.

There is much more to sports than offense and defense. But what in the world does sports—especially offense and defense—have to do with prayer? Let's transfer the idea of offense and defense from a sports point of view to a prayer point of view.

PRAYER OFFENSE AND DEFENSE

Let's look at a few hypothetical examples. Assume Brent has just lost his job. Or assume Ashley has just found out she has a serious health condition. Or assume Milton and Jean are struggling in their marriage and have separated with no desire to reconcile. In these three situations it is "crunch" time for these folks. They are losing the ball game. They're down. It's late in the game. It doesn't appear at all as if there is victory in store for them. It's looking like defeat.

What do we do as their friends and family at this point? We pinch-hit for them. We go to bat for them, intercede for them, and step up our "prayer defense." We hunker down in prayer and give it all we've got in prayer on their behalf because we don't want them to lose the ball game. So we step up our "prayer defense." We haven't prayed for them on any other occasion. As a matter of fact, it can even be said that we only pray for them in "crunch" time or crisis time. And it is in these times when we pray for them in "defensive mode."

Is that wrong? Is that bad? No! We will all face struggles and difficult challenges in our lives. We absolutely need others to go to bat for us, to intercede for us. We need people who will step up their "prayer defense" when it's late in the ball game and we are losing at this game called life.

But what would happen if we prayed for each other along life's journey in an "offensive" mode? What if we stepped up our "prayer offense"? What if we had been praying regularly for Brent and his job for the last year? What if we had been praying for Ashley for the last year or two for her health? What if we had been lifting our friends Milton and Jean regularly in prayer for the last several years, praying for a God-centered, God-honoring, solid marriage?

As I stated before, if the offense would actually work harder and score some points and victories along the way, the defense wouldn't have to work so hard when it's crunch time. "Prayer offense." I'll admit it's a different way of looking at prayer. But it makes sense. And this is exactly the way the Apostle Paul prayed for the church at Colossae.

PAUL'S PRAYER OFFENSE

Paul had never met the Christians in Colossae before. He was under house arrest in Rome at the time he wrote this letter. The church in Colossae had some issues and struggles that Paul addressed in his letter to them. However, he didn't pray for them in defense mode. He didn't say "I'm going to pray you through this crisis or hard time." He prayed for them in offense mode.

First of all it's important to note that even though Paul had never visited the Colossians, he said to them "We always pray for you..." (Colossians 1:3, NLT). Isn't that cool? He was constantly praying for a group of Christians that he'd never laid eyes on. He continued, saying:

> [9]...so you will understand that since we heard about you we have never missed you in our prayers. We are asking God that you may see things, as it were, from his point of view by being given spiritual insight and understanding. [10]We also pray that your outward lives, which men see, may bring credit to your master's name, and that you may bring joy to his heart by bearing genuine Christian fruit, and that your knowledge of God may grow yet deeper. [11]As you live this new life, we pray that you will be strengthened from God's boundless resources, so that you will find

yourselves able to pass through any experience and endure it with courage. ¹²You will even be able to thank God in the midst of pain and distress because you are privileged to share the lot of those who are living in the light.

(Colossians 1:9-12, JB Phillips)

Go back and reread that first sentence. Paul's first response, upon hearing about the Colossians, was to pray for them. Praying for people isn't necessarily our first response, is it? When we hear about a situation or circumstance in someone's life, we frequently respond by doing: helping, serving, giving, etc. Our church participates frequently with Habitat for Humanity. Upon the building of a new home, some in our church respond by going to the site and physically picking up tools to build. Some respond by volunteering to go serve lunch. Others respond by donating money or building materials. We respond to the needs of others in a variety of ways. Neither helping, serving, nor giving was Paul's first response to the Christians at Colossae. Paul's first response was to pray for them.

Paul modeled beautifully for us what it means to be on "prayer offense." His prayer contains seven things that we can and should pray for each other on a regular basis.

OUR PRAYER IN ACTION

First, pray that others may see things from God's point of view (v. 9). Paul prayed that the folks in Colossae would have a complete understanding of what God wanted to accomplish in their lives. He prayed that they would understand the will of God for them. Would you like to see things from God's point of view? To understand God's will for your life? To see through His eyes? If we had this ability, I think we would look at people differently. We would look at situations

118

differently. If we had an understanding of what God wanted to accomplish in us and through us we would act differently, think differently, and speak differently. How exciting it would be to see things from God's point of view!

Next, pray that others may be given spiritual insight and understanding (v. 9). Some translations of the Bible call it (spiritual insight) wisdom. Recall James 3:17: "But the wisdom that comes from heaven is first of all pure; then peace-loving, considerate, submissive, full of mercy and good fruit, impartial and sincere." This is a constant prayer of my own. When I am struggling through a difficult time, seeking God's will for my life in certain circumstances, I turn this verse into a prayer so that God will reveal to me how to act, react, think, behave, what to say, and how to proceed. I want and need the "wisdom that comes from heaven" in my life. Paul prayed for spiritual insight to be given to the Colossians so that they, too, would know how to live.

Third, pray that the outward lives of others may bring credit to the Master's name (v. 10). If our outward lives— what we do and say—would indeed bring honor and glory to God, non-Christians would take notice. I can't help but believe that if everything we did truly brought credit to the Master's name, we would immediately draw attention away from us and toward our Heavenly Father. People would absolutely take notice of that. It would open for us many opportunities to candidly share who we are in Christ Jesus. We, ourselves, ought to accept this as a personal challenge as we pray for others to do the same.

Next, pray for others to bring joy to God's heart by bearing genuine Christian fruit (v. 10). How badly do you want your loved ones to bring joy to God's heart? How badly do *you* want to bring joy to God's heart? If bearing genuine Christian fruit is what it takes to bring joy to God's heart, then we ought to be praying for that regularly for our Christian brothers and sisters as well as ourselves. If we are not growing spiritually, we are not bearing fruit. If we are not growing spiritually or bearing fruit, then what does that do to God's heart? I believe Paul, more than most, had a pretty good understanding of God's heart. Paul understood what Jesus meant when He told His disciples ". . . I chose you and appointed you to go and bear fruit—fruit that will last" (John 15:16). Unfortunately, I see so many Christians today who are not staying close enough to the Vine to bear genuine Christian fruit. Please pray for those in your midst to be fruit bearers who bring joy to God.

When interceding for others, pray that their knowledge of God may grow yet deeper (v. 10). Pray that your friends and family would know Christ—deeper, more personally, more intimately. Not know *about* God, but *know* God. Don't be impressed by those who know stories of the Bible, or can list the books of the Bible in correct order, or even by those who warm the pew next to you each week. Pray that their knowledge of God would grow deeper and deeper.

One of the things I would love to do is scuba dive. Unfortunately, I grew up with a history of ear problems. So for me to dive down very deeply is extremely painful. But I'd love to be able to swim down to the deep parts of the sea and look at all the cool things that God has created—the colorful fish, the coral, rock formations, and other beautiful sea creatures. I have even dreamed of finding buried treasure as I explore the ocean floor. In order to find that treasure, however, I would have to work at getting that deep. I'd have to kick my legs and pull with my arms and swim with effort to reach that deep point. If I just floated I would stay on the surface.

Paul didn't want the Colossians to be "surface" Christians. He wanted them to work at being deeper Christians. Why? Because that's where the treasure is—the treasure of a deeper knowledge of the Almighty God!

Next, pray for strength and endurance for other people in your life (v. 11). Pray for strength and endurance for this journey that we call faith; strength and endurance for this journey that we call the Christian walk. Pray that your friends and family would have power and stamina through the many struggles that they will face. Many trials require a great deal of strength and endurance. Score some points along the journey by praying that God would build these traits in those that you know and love.

Finally, pray for others to be able to thank God in the midst of pain and distress (v. 12). Remember what James said about trials and temptations? He said "Consider it pure joy, my brothers, whenever you face trials of many kinds..." (James 1:2). Look closer. He said "when," not "if." You see, God's people are not exempt from having struggles and challenges. We will face hard times. We will struggle. But if we pray offensively for our friends and family, then when struggles come they will be able to experience joy somewhere in the midst of those struggles.

MIGHT THERE BE MORE?

As I stated earlier, Paul gave us a wonderful model in Colossians 1:9-12 of what to pray for other people. But Paul realized that he needed to be prayed for as well. In the final chapter of Colossians he included a few requests of his own:

> ²Always maintain the habit of prayer: be both alert and thankful as you pray. ³Include us in your prayers, please, that God may open for us a door for the entrance of the Gospel. Pray that we may talk freely of the mystery of Christ (for which I am at present in chains), ⁴and that I may make that mystery plain to men, which I know is my duty.
>
> (Colossians 4:2-4, JB Phillips)

Paul knew that prayer was not meant to be one-sided. He knew the power of praying for each other. He made two simple prayer requests of the Colossians. He asked them to *pray for an open door to share Christ* and *to share Him clearly (v. 3)*. Paul felt strongly that this was his duty—to share openly the Good News of Jesus Christ with other people. This was his calling. This was his delight.

As devoted followers of Jesus Christ we cannot leave these same prayer requests out of our offense. When we pray for other Christians we must include these same prayers. Not only was it Paul's duty to share Jesus Christ with others, but it is ours too. And if we are going to share Christ effectively with non-Christians, we certainly need to be bathed in prayer by our brothers and sisters in Christ. And if being in Christ, or being a part of the family of God, is such a big deal to us, then why aren't we sharing that Good News with others more often? If we were to pray more fervently for one another for open doors and opportunities to share Christ clearly with non-Christians, we would be much more effective in furthering the Kingdom of God.

A PROFOUND GREETING

Paul finished his letter to the Christians at Colossae with a few final greetings. I cannot overlook one key greeting while we are discussing the subject of praying for others. Locked away in chapter four is one key verse. "Epaphras, who is one of you and a servant of Christ Jesus, sends greetings. He is always wrestling in prayer for you, that you may stand firm in all the will of God, mature and fully assured" (Colossians 4:12). Epaphras, a "much loved co-worker" of Paul's (Colossians 1:7, NLT), brought the Good News to the people of Colossae. He is thought to be the one responsible for starting the church there. But catch what Paul said about him in regards to prayer: "He is always wrestling in prayer for you..." In the New American Standard Version, Paul describes Epaphras as "always laboring earnestly for you in his prayers." The words "wrestling" and "laboring" in the original Greek come from the word *agonizomai* which means to contend, to fight, to endeavor with strenuous zeal. From this Greek word we get our word "agonize." Epaphras agonized in prayer for these people. He "labored fervently" (NKJV). He "struggled on their behalf" (ESV). He "prayed hard" (CEV).

It is so easy to pray simple prayers for each other like "please bless Lance" or "please help Isabella." But if we are serious about getting in the game—serious about going to bat for others, interceding on their behalf—then we need to pray differently. If we would actually wrestle in prayer for each other, if we would increase our "prayer offense," I believe God would unleash His power to accomplish great things in us and through us. And we would be able to sit alongside our friends, family, co-workers, etc. and watch God be glorified because we had the privilege of praying for them!

MAKING IT REAL

1. In the words of the apostle Paul, "maintain a habit of prayer" this week for someone in your world. Pray for them every day.
2. Who in your life do you need to "wrestle in prayer" for? Your spouse, kids, coworkers, neighbors, small group? Pick a few of those dear people. Pray for the things that I mentioned in this chapter for them. And enjoy watching God go to work!
3. Take a moment to thank God for the privilege we have to "go to bat" for others. We don't *have* to pray for other people . . . we *get* to!
4. Take a moment to thank God for those who have "gone to bat" for you. If you are reading this book

right now as a fully devoted follower of Jesus Christ, it is because someone cared enough about you and invested time praying for you. Thank God for them. And if you have the courage, thank them personally.

9

Praying For Yourself
(1 Samuel 1:10-11; 1 Kings 3:6-9)

I was flying to Chicago recently on an early morning flight. My anticipation of the trip and my desire not to over sleep caused me not to sleep well the night before. So, on the flight I decided to do something that I never do. I decided to recline my seat back so I could try to relax and perhaps rest. The reason I never do this is simple—I feel guilty for being selfish and I feel badly for the people behind me who have the back of my seat in their face or their tray table launched into their gut. Nevertheless, on this early morning, I was going to "put me first." In an effort not to appear too greedy, I decided to nonchalantly reach my hand down to press the button to recline my seat ever so tenderly. I gently pushed. Nothing happened. I pressed a little harder and gave some force with my back and legs this time, expecting to glide back subtly and begin my relaxation. I didn't even budge. My seat remained upright. But out of the corner of my eye, to my amazement and embarrassment, the gentleman sitting next to me abruptly shot backwards. Oops! I pushed the wrong button. He unexpectedly was reclining while I was still sitting upright. I awkwardly looked over at him and said, "I just wanted you to be comfortable for the flight."

There are times when we put *ourselves* first. Sometimes we want to. Sometimes the situation warrants that we must—like placing the oxygen mask on yourself first in an airplane emergency before assisting others. Sometimes putting ourselves first comes naturally—wanting to be the first in line, choosing the best seat in the theater, etc. But, now and then we actually have to work at putting ourselves ahead of everyone else. For example when we moms are sick and should be in bed taking care of ourselves, we are usually up continuing the role of "Super Mom"—cooking, cleaning, getting the kids ready for school, etc.

Alternatively, there are times when we do for *others* first—we do what's expected in polite society. Again, some of the time it's part of our training—letting a friend have the last cookie on the plate, holding the door open for someone else at the grocery store, etc. But occasionally it's not natural, and we actually have to work at that too.

My son Caleb, who was nine years old at the time, was sitting beside me during a Sunday morning worship service at our church. He rummaged through my purse looking for some candy (which is typical for my sons during church). I was half paying attention to him and half trying to sing. Within about a minute he leaned over and, without words, offered me the mint in his hand. I remember thinking, "This is a momentous occasion because my son just offered me the *first* mint. He's actually beginning to understand the principle of putting others first. How very cool!" I graciously said "thank you," popped the mint into my mouth and continued to worship with a smile on my face feeling very proud of my first born. But that feeling only lasted about thirty seconds. That's when he leaned over and whispered to me, "That mint fell on the floor and I didn't know what to do with it." I thought he had a genuine breakthrough moment. But no . . . a mother can only hope...

As we go through life there are many occasions in which we put other people's needs above our own. Often times this is all we know. It is what has been engrained in us since birth. The thought of actually doing something for ourselves is either foreign to us or perhaps for some it even borders on being wrong.

PRAYER INSTINCTS

But what about praying? Is that something we instinctively or naturally do for ourselves? Do we have to work at it? Is it really acceptable to pray for ourselves? Are we only to pray for other people? I am amazed at the number of people in my life who openly confess that they pray for other people all the time, but seldom or never pray for themselves because it doesn't feel right to do so. "It just seems too selfish," they say. Or "There are so many other people and other situations to pray for, I just can't get myself to pray for ME."

This may come as a surprise to you, but the pages of Scripture are loaded with people praying for themselves. Jacob did it (Genesis 32), Hezekiah did it (2 Kings 19), Jabez did it (1 Chronicles 4), David did it (Psalm 4), Jesus did it (John 17), and Paul did it (2 Corinthians 12)—just to name a few. If these people, including Jesus, prayed for themselves, shouldn't we follow their example?

HANNAH AND SOLOMON

Let's look at two people in the Old Testament who prayed for themselves. Not only did they pray for themselves, but they did so with passion and fervor. Both went to the Lord in prayer at very critical times in their lives.

Hannah, one of the two wives of Elkanah, was child-less. Elkanah's other wife Peninnah had children and "made fun of Hannah because the LORD had closed her womb" (1 Samuel 1:6, NLT). The taunting went on year after year. Hannah was desperate.

> [10] In bitterness of soul Hannah wept much and prayed to the LORD. [11]And she made a vow, saying, "O LORD Almighty, if you will only look upon your servant's misery and remember me, and not forget your servant but give her a son, then I will give him to the LORD for all the days of his life, and no razor will ever be used on his head."
>
> (1 Samuel 1:10-11)

Now, let's pause here and consider another Old Testament figure, Solomon. Solomon was the son of King David and the heir to the throne. (Large shoes to fill for Solomon because David was not only a great king but a "man after God's own heart.") When Solomon first took the throne, God appeared to him and asked, "What do you want? Ask and I will give it to you."

> [6]Solomon answered, "You have shown great kindness to your servant, my father David, because he was faithful to you and righteous and upright in heart. You have continued this great kindness to him and have given him a son to sit on his throne this very day.
> [7]"Now, O LORD my God, you have made your servant king in place of my father David. But I am only a little child and do not know how to carry out my duties. [8]Your servant is here among the people you have chosen, a great people, too numerous to count or number. [9] So give your servant a discerning heart

to govern your people and to distinguish between right and wrong. For who is able to govern this great people of yours?"

(1 Kings 3:6-9)

These two prayers could not be more different, yet at the same time, could not be more alike. They came from vastly different people. One prayer from a childless woman—another from a child king. Eventually this woman's son would anoint this king's father as king of Israel. Both knew the God of Abraham, Isaac, and Jacob. And both cried out in prayer to this same God of their ancestors . . . the same God who hears us today. Both took the time and effort to pray for a specific personal need or desire. What, then, can we learn from these two different people who prayed in similar ways?

PERSONAL PRAYER

First, when Hannah and Solomon approached God, they did so with great humility. They both refer to themselves as "servants." Even Solomon, king over Israel, called himself a servant in his prayer. They both knew, recognized, and appreciated the sovereignty of God. They knew their standing before the Almighty God. And the only way to approach Him with a request was with the attitude of humility and servanthood. They seemed to be saying to God, "I serve You. You don't serve me. I know where I stand." Oh, that we could approach God in this same way. Oh, that we could grasp the vastness and infiniteness and greatness of our God. Our only response, then, would be to come to Him in unassuming humility.

Next, they both made their desire known to God. Again, Hannah and Solomon went to the Lord at critical times in their lives. Hannah desperately wanted a child. Solomon desperately wanted to be a great king. Both of them knew exactly what they wanted God to do for them . . . so they asked Him. They simply *asked* God for what they wanted. Recall in Chapter 4, when we're facing a crisis, I encouraged us to be specific when we pray. The same thing applies here. When Hannah and Solomon made their desires known to God, they were very specific in what they asked God for. Don't be afraid to be specific with our great big God when you make your desires known to Him.

We are exhorted to do the same thing by the Apostle Paul. "Be anxious for nothing, but in everything by prayer and supplication with thanksgiving let your requests be made known to God" (Philippians 4:6, NAS). Did you see that? In the NLT Paul stated "Tell God what you need." It is right there in the Word of God that we are to pray for ourselves.

Finally, their requests were not for selfish gain. They did not ask God for something entirely to please themselves. As a matter of fact, Hannah said, "Lord, if you give me a son, I'll give him back to You." How unselfish was that? Yes, Hannah very much wanted a son. She very much wanted to rid herself of the stigma that came with being childless. She very much wanted to put an end to the constant mocking and name-calling. But she had a deeper understanding of what the gift of a son would bring. She understood that the blessing of a son to her would also turn into a blessing not only for the Lord, but ultimately for other people. That's humility at its finest. That's a servant's heart. That's the epitome of altruism.

Solomon, a relatively young king, said, "God, give me a discerning heart so that I may govern Your people." In other words, Solomon said, "I need Your help with what You have given me. I want to be able to distinguish right and wrong so I can govern Your people." He recognized he was in a position of leadership, and he wanted to lead well so God's people would follow well. Was that self-centered? Sounds to me like it was "others-centered." His focus was not as much on himself as it was on the people he was governing. He wanted the gift of wisdom so that he could use it for God's glory.

Were they bargaining with God? Were they playing "Let's Make A Deal"? Were they manipulating God in some way? I don't think so. It actually symbolized how *unselfish* they were. Their hearts and motives were pure. Hannah did not keep the son she was blessed with. "After he was weaned, she took the boy with her, young as he was . . . and brought him to the house of the LORD" (1 Samuel 1:24). She brought the boy before Eli the priest and said, "I prayed for this child, and the LORD has granted me what I asked of him. So now I give him to the LORD. For his whole life he will be given over to the LORD" (1 Samuel 1:27-28a).

Solomon did not gain wisdom and discernment and store it all up for himself. He used this gift. He exercised the blessing he was given. And the people he governed "held the king in awe, because they saw that he had wisdom from God to administer justice" (1 Kings 3:28b).

Both Hannah and Solomon gave away the blessing that they received from God. God had been working in both of their lives up to this point. He was preparing them to be blessed and use that blessing for far greater things than they could imagine. God is not capable of being manipulated or bargained with. He simply gave Hannah and Solomon what they asked for. He gave them the desires of their hearts. He desires to do the same for us.

EXCUSES, EXCUSES, EXCUSES

So what is your excuse for not praying for yourself? You're too busy? (Here we go again!) You don't want to be selfish because there are so many other people who need prayer? It doesn't occur to you to spend time praying for yourself? Maybe you think it's too much responsibility to pray for yourself. Too much pressure? What if God answers your prayer, then will He expect something from you in return?

Any excuse for not praying for yourself is like putting God in a box. When you do not pray for yourself you are placing limits on the Almighty God. How's that, you might say?

Let's look at two hypothetical examples. Juan has two young children that he absolutely adores. He loves it when they come to him with little problems they need help solving, bumps and bruises for him to kiss, exciting stories of their day they want to share with him, etc. He treasures the moments when he gets to dry their tears, or offer them a smile and a hug when they've experienced something unpleasant. What if Juan's children never came to him for any of those things? His role as daddy would become limited. He would be confined and restricted from the things he longs to give them.

Similarly, Paula is a dear friend to several women in her neighborhood and workplace. She has a genuine servant's heart as she listens to their struggles, offers a shoulder to cry on, gives encouragement when she can, and helps out with babysitting or car rides when her friends are in a jam. She thoroughly loves serving her friends when she's given the opportunity. But what if they never gave her that opportunity? What if they never asked her advice, needed a shoulder to cry on, or came to her in a jam? Paula would be denied the things she loves to do. Her role as friend would be confined and restricted from what she wanted to give her friends.

Transfer these two scenarios to you and God. When you do not pray for yourself you are denying God His heart's desire to meet your need, to provide for you, to bless you, to comfort you, to give you peace, to carry you through a tough time in your life, etc.

NOT YET CONVINCED?

So, have I convinced you yet? Are you feeling the urge to sit down right now and do some praying for yourself? If not, consider a few more encouraging (or challenging) words from God's Word:

Psalm 37:4 reads, "Delight yourself in the Lord and he will give you the desires of your heart." Did you catch that? *Delight* yourself! Have you ever invited special guests to your home? You cook, clean the house, mow the yard, and get things "just so." And as the time of their arrival draws nearer you become more and more excited. There is an internal energy brewing within you. You anticipate the moment when they first pull into your driveway...heart pounding when you hear the doorbell ring. You hurry to the door to greet them—perhaps with a big smile or a long embrace. You can't wait for them to step into your home. You're eager to meet with them, to share your life with them, and to listen to them share theirs. In this same way, we need to get excited and anticipate our opportunities to spend time with God. After all, He is so eager to meet with us. He wants to share His life with us and longs for us to share our lives with Him. Choose to delight yourself in the Lord!

James 4:2b-3 brings to us this challenging thought: "You do not have, because you do not ask God. When you ask, you do not receive, because you ask with wrong motives, that you may spend what you get on your pleasures." Wow! Could it be that you don't have peace inside because you've never asked for it. Maybe you're struggling to reconcile a relationship because you haven't asked for God's help. Maybe you're not experiencing any joy in your relationship with Jesus Christ because you haven't asked God to give you joy in knowing Him. Whatever current challenge or circumstance you are facing, have you truly asked God to be in the center of it? And have you asked with right motive and a pure heart? If you're not sure if your motives are right or your heart is pure in what you ask, then ask God to help you clarify that. Ask a dear Christian friend or pastor to prayer- fully investigate your motives with you. Both Hannah and Solomon had pure motives and right hearts. And God chose to bless them because of it.

Perhaps Matthew 6:33 will encourage you to pray for yourself: "But seek first his kingdom and his righteousness, and all these things will be given to you as well." In this verse there are two essentials—"seek" and "first!" Seeking requires action on our part. Seek first! First God, then your- self. God first in your focus, first in your desire, and first in your motive. Make God first.

Consider the words of the Apostle John in John 15:7: "If you remain in me and my words remain in you, ask what- ever you wish, and it will be given you." Can we just go and do things our own way, in our own time, in our own effort and then go to God in a jam and say, "Hey, can you help me out here?" Jesus' first request here was to *remain* in Him. Remain! Stay put! Linger! Hang around! Not come and go like a quick trip to the convenience store. But remain! His second request was that His words remain in you. His teach- ings need to take up residence in our hearts. His Word needs to dwell in us. Oh, that God's children would just embrace this verse. Embrace the truth of it. Embrace the invitation of it. God would delight in us—I'm sure of it!

JOY IN THE JOURNEY

When we finally do begin praying for ourselves, we must be careful not to get our eyes set on the destination or the end result of the answer to our prayer. When we commit this error we have missed out on the journey. Yes, there is great fulfill- ment in the *answer* of prayer, but there is also great joy in the *journey* of prayer. There are many lessons to learn as we pray through a need and trust God all along the way. There is joy to be had along the journey. If Hannah were around today to talk about her experience, I believe she would say, "Yes, that period of my life was the most miserable period I ever had . . . but I wouldn't trade it for the world. It caused me to be on my knees; it caused me to cry out to God; it allowed me to be in such wonderful communion with God . . . and I was never the same again!" Hannah's focus was more on God than on the goal.

I'll ask the question again . . . Have I convinced you yet? Cool! So, where do you start?

MAKING IT PERSONAL

There is no better place to begin than with the prayers of the Apostle Paul. This man prayed fervently for the people of Ephesus, Philippi, Colossae, and so many others. Most of his prayers were prayed while in prison. Dark times for this zealous man of God, yet wonderful times spent in prayer for those his heart went out to. Through his example of praying for other people, we can compile a wonderful list of prayers to pray for ourselves.

A great place to begin praying for yourself is to *pray that you will know God better.* I wrote about this same thing in the previous chapter when we addressed what to pray for other people. It's the same prayer for us here, although it comes from a different letter of Paul's. His prayer in Ephesians 1:17 reads, "I keep asking that the God of our Lord Jesus Christ, the glorious Father, may give you the Spirit of wisdom and revelation, so that you may know him better." Relationships work better when we know each other better. We should pray that we would know God better. Not know *about* Him; but really *know* Him!

Next, pray that the eyes of your heart would be enlightened. From this same prayer of Paul's in verse 18 he said,

"I pray also that the eyes of your heart may be enlightened in order that you may know the hope to which he has called you..." Pray that the eyes of your heart would be opened, awakened, and fully accessible to God. It is our hearts that need to know Him better. We need to move the knowledge from our heads to our hearts so that we actually live out what we say we believe. Birthed out of the heart are things like love, compassion, sincerity, empathy, kindness, gentleness, generosity, concern, etc. When our hearts are enlightened by God, and become engaged with these godly characteristics, then we are moved to act out these characteristics. The trans-ference from head knowledge to heart awakening breeds action and a Christian life that's not only thought about, but lived out.

Third, pray to discern what is best. Philippians 1:9-10 reads, "And this is my prayer: that your love may abound more and more in knowledge and depth of insight, so that you may be able to discern what is best and may be pure and blameless until the day of Christ..." This is essentially what King Solomon prayed. He wanted the ability to discern between right and wrong. Friends, we need this discernment as well. People of the 21st century have mastered the art of living in the "gray areas." They adhere to a belief system where there is no black and white. They soften the blow of their sinful living by claiming that there are no moral abso-lutes. God's Word is absolute. God's Word is truth. In His Word, He tells us what is right and what is wrong. We need to pray like Solomon who "did not know how to carry out his duties." We, like Solomon, need discernment.

Fourth, pray that you would walk in obedience. Solomon's father, King David, prayed this in Psalm 143:10, "Teach me to do your will, for you are my God; may your good Spirit lead me on level ground." Pray that you would say "yes" to God without hesitation and regardless of the cost. "Take all your present perplexities to the Lord. Tell Him you only want to know and obey His voice, and ask Him to make it plain to you. Promise Him that you will obey, whatever it may be."[1]

The next two come from Paul's letter to the Colossians. *First, pray that you would please Him in every way.* Colossians 1:10 reads, "And we pray this in order that you may live a life worthy of the Lord and may please him in every way: bearing fruit in every good work, growing in the knowledge of God..." Pray that everything you do, everything you say, everything you think would be glorifying to God. Our hearts should want to please God's heart with our whole being.

Next, in that same verse, pray that you would bear fruit. Do you know the difference between a perennial plant and an annual plant? An annual plant only lasts for one season. You may plant them in the spring, they will produce beautiful flowers all summer long, but by fall they're done. They're dead. No more beautiful flowers. You pull them out and toss them aside.

A perennial, on the other hand, produces its flowers in season. But it doesn't quit there. It doesn't have one shining moment in its life and then retire. It comes back season after season, producing more flowers each year; growing bigger and better year after year. We are called to bear fruit. And to keep bearing fruit. I don't know about you, but I don't want to be a "one-timer," an annual, who bears fruit for God in only one season, then gets plucked out and tossed aside. I want to be a consistent fruit-bearer for God. I want to be better this year than I was last year. I want people to stop and take notice of the fruit that I bear so they can say, "Wow! Look what God is doing in her life!"

And finally, pray that you would be filled to the measure of the fullness of God. Paul prayed in Ephesians 3:19 that those in Ephesus would know the love of Christ "that (they)

137

may be filled to the measure of all the fullness of God." I love this verse. Let me explain why:

Imagine for a moment that in front of you is a clear plastic cup sitting on a table. This cup represents YOU. There is a line about a fourth of the way up from the bottom. Now imagine also on the table a pitcher full of water. This pitcher represents GOD. Up to this point you have only prayed for yourself a few times. You have only asked for a small amount from God (because it would be selfish to ask for more, right?). So, God (the water pitcher) pours just enough water into your cup to equal the mark toward the bottom.

Now imagine there are several other clear plastic cups on the table as well. One is marked "family," one is marked "job," one is marked "church responsibilities," one is marked "little league coach," one is marked "PTA," etc. So, you take the cup that represents YOU and begin to pour a little of your water into the cup labeled "family." Then you pour from your cup a little of your water into the cup marked "job," and then pour into "church," etc. You know that you need to "pour yourself into" these other areas of your life. You need to and you want to. However, if you have very little water in your cup to begin with, the cups that you're pouring into get even less. They get just a dollop of you. Do you see the problem? But if you're "filled to the measure of all the fullness of God" then you have plenty of water from your cup to pour into the others. God's water supply into your cup is never ending . . . if only you ask for it! Pray that you would be filled to the measure of the fullness of God!

I am convinced, friends, that if God's people would pray for themselves with such abandon as Hannah and Solomon and others in the Scriptures, there is no telling what the body of Christ could accomplish for God's glory! My friends, you have a transformation waiting for you if you would just ask God for it. How about starting right now?

MAKING IT REAL

1. Give yourself the green light to pray for yourself this week.
2. Which portions of Paul's prayers do you need to begin praying for yourself starting today? Write those down. Put them in a place that you'll see frequently throughout the day so that you'll be reminded to pray for God to work on you often.
3. Consider two or three specific needs in your life (personal, emotional, spiritual, professional, physical, etc.). Take those requests to our Heavenly Father.
4. Keep your eyes open . . . and watch God go to work on you!

10

Fellowship On Fire
(Acts 1:13-14; 2:42; 6:4)

Earthquakophobia. Cancerophobia. Electrophobia. Arsonophobia. It almost sounds like I'm making these up, but I'm not. These phobias are real. You can probably figure them out just from the names. Fear of earthquakes, fear of cancer, fear of electricity, and fear of fire. How about these: arachnophobia, claustrophobia, agoraphobia. That list is more commonly known. They are the fear of spiders, the fear of enclosed spaces, and the fear of open spaces, respectively.

I read through a list of phobias once and I had no idea there were that many. I suppose if someone has a legitimate fear of something, the "experts" have to identify it then give it an official name. And honestly, as I read through the list I kept thinking that someone was inventing them. They borderlined on the absurd and ridiculous, but I quickly had to remind myself that there are probably as many phobias as there are situations or circumstances. People have genuine fears of many things. The things that you and I would consider quite normal or basic or boring, some folks actually fear. For instance, did you know that some people are truly afraid of balloons? This is known as globophobia. The fear of clothing is called vestiphobia. Some people suffer from octophobia. It is the fear of the figure 8. The fear of knees is known as genuphobia. And what does one fear if they have hippophobia? No, not hippos. It's actually the fear of horses.

A PHOBIA AMONG CHRISTIANS

In the entire list, however, I did not see a phobia that is common to many Christians today. We see this fear in church, in Bible studies, in Sunday school classes, in small groups, in public and in private. This fear affects men and women, young and old. It isn't specific to any race or color of skin. It is genuine. It is legitimate. What is this mysterious fear that plagues many Christians today? It is the fear of praying out loud in front of other people. Maybe we should give it an official name. Perhaps we could call the fear of praying out loud "verbaprayerophobia" or "oralintercessophobia." Whatever we call it there are many who would claim to have it.

I have spoken to so many Christians who really struggle with praying out loud in front of other people. They say it's embarrassing or intimidating. They are too self-conscious. "What if I mess up?" "What if I say something stupid?" "What if I can't find the right words?" "I get tongue-tied." "I can't pray as eloquently as other people." The excuses go on and on.

I like to challenge those folks with the thought that talking to God is like talking to me. It's just a conversation. If we fear that our prayer won't impress anyone, then our hearts are in the wrong place. If we fear that we might say something stupid, then our focus isn't in the right place. Prayer is simply about you and our Heavenly Father. He doesn't care if it is formal or informal, short or lengthy, impressive or simple. He just wants to hear from us!

I went to a prayer meeting once where the leader started out by saying, "Well, God, here we are!" I almost laughed out loud. Not because it was wrong or inappropriate or funny—but because it was joyfully casual and refreshingly genuine. It was truly the essence of what a conversation with God looked like. It was wonderful. She immediately took away the preconception of a "formal" prayer setting and made everyone feel at home in the presence of God.

AN OPPORTUNITY UNTAKEN

Now, I would like for you to hold that thought for a moment while we take a look at some passages of Scripture. Recall in Chapter 2, we looked at the passage in which Jesus took Peter, James, and John to the garden of Gethsemane (Matthew 26:36-44). This was shortly before His arrest. He asked them to pray while He went off by Himself to pray as well. When He came back, He didn't find them praying. They were sleeping. So He asked them a second time to pray. When He returned He found the same thing—no praying, just sleeping. And the same thing occurred a third time. They were instructed to spend some time praying but they fell incredibly short.

Was it that they were afraid to pray out loud with each other? Was that altogether too awkward for them? Did they, like many of us, suffer from "verbaprayerophobia"? I seriously doubt they were afraid to pray out loud in front of each other, but nonetheless it didn't happen. They missed out on a powerful opportunity to spend time in prayer with each other. We'll look more at this later in the chapter, but when we gather together in prayer, we are in the presence of God. Peter, James, and John could have spent time "touching and agreeing" (as some people would say) in God's company, but instead they chose sleep.

AN OPPORTUNITY TAKEN

Now, fast forward to the passage in Acts 1:13-14. Luke recorded that "When they arrived, they went upstairs to the room where they were staying. Those present were Peter, John, James and Andrew; Philip and Thomas, Bartholomew and Matthew; James son of Alphaeus and Simon the Zealot, and Judas son of James. They all joined together constantly in prayer, along with the women and Mary the mother of Jesus, and with his brothers." Did you catch who was listed among those who "joined together constantly in prayer"? This was the same Peter, James, and John who several weeks prior failed when given the opportunity to pray together— even at the Master's request. Yet there they were in Acts 1:14 "continually devoting themselves to prayer" (NAS).

What happened to them? Did they have a change of heart? A change of priority? Did guilt get the best of them when they missed a golden opportunity earlier? Perhaps it was their encounter with the risen Lord and His glorious ascension into heaven that brought about change. It's hard to say. The point is they were noticeably different in the first chapter of Acts than they were in the Garden of Gethsemane in Matthew 26.

DEVOTED!

Thirty-four times in the book of Acts (in the NIV) some form of the word "pray" occurs. Eighteen out of the 34 times, the word "pray" or "prayed" or "praying" is linked with a group or a pair of people. As a matter of fact, this group of first-century Christians was "continually devoting themselves to the apostles' teaching and to fellowship, to the breaking of bread and to prayer" (Acts 2:42, NAS). Further, the Twelve gathered all the followers of Christ together and told them of their intent to give their "attention to prayer and the ministry of the word" (Acts 6:4, NAS).

The phrase "They were continually devoting themselves," believe it or not, is one word in the Greek. *Proskartereo* implies an adherence to or a steadfast attentiveness to. It means to continue all the time in a place or to persist. That was their attitude toward prayer—to adhere to it, to be steadfastly attentive to it, to pursue it persistently. Not only that, but it was their attitude toward three additional disciplines that are essential to the Church today.

I'll never forget what Bill Hybels, pastor of Willowcreek Church, once said. While attending a conference there I heard him say, "There's nothing like the Church when the Church is working right!" That sentence hasn't left me since.

Acts 2:42 is a snapshot of the Church working right. If we could freeze that moment in time and bring it forward to today, I guarantee the Church would look quite differently than it does now. I honestly wonder what most churches are really devoted to. I fear that many churches today are more devoted to programs, not prayer. I'm concerned that churches today are more devoted to dollars, not discipleship. I worry that many churches today have been sidetracked by technology, and not devoted to teaching the Word of God. If that is indeed true, then we are not only missing the mark but also missing out!

Look again at the verse. "They devoted themselves to the apostles' teaching and to the fellowship, to the breaking of bread and to prayer" (Acts 2:42). There they are again—the four essentials for the Church to embrace today.

First, they devoted themselves to the apostles teaching. They sat at the apostles' feet and were hungry for instruction. They were hungry for a deeper knowledge of this amazing God we have. Are we as hungry for this same instruction and deeper knowledge of God? Are *you*? If we were truly hungry for the Word of God our church services would be full, our Sunday school classes would be standing room only, and our weekly Bible studies would be packed full of eager people ready to hear and apply the Word of God. Unfortunately, many churches do not have this problem. For many, church is a one hour per week event. Devotion to teaching goes beyond hearing a twenty minute sermon once a week. Devotion to teaching should include disciplines such as Sunday school, small group Bible studies, personal Bible study, listening to or reading books by great Christian speakers, teachers, and authors.

Second, they devoted themselves to fellowship. The word for fellowship in the Greek is *koinonia* which indicates sharing something in common, a partnership, participation with one another, and communication. I have noticed something in the last several years. Something sad and unfortunate really. I have noticed that when we get together with Christian friends socially, the one thing we most have in common with each other is the least talked about. We frequently come from different backgrounds, social status, race, and such. Sometimes we are noticeably different than each other. But as Christians, the one thing we all have in common is our personal relationship with Jesus Christ. This fact makes us nothing less than brothers and sisters in Him. However, you'd never know we had that in common because we rarely talk about it when we get together. We talk about the weather, our jobs, politics, our kids, the local sports teams, etc. Rarely do we ask each other how we are doing spiritually or what God is teaching us lately. We talk about church stuff. But that doesn't count—it's mostly gossip anyway. If you don't believe me, pay attention the next time you get together for dinner with some Christian friends. Take note of the conversation. Be aware of your fellowship together. Were you encouraged in your faith at all? Did anyone even care to ask? Be intentional about your fellowship with friends, family, coworkers, neighbors, etc. Encourage others in their faith, and be encouraged in yours. Intentionally ask people what God is doing in their lives. Direct the conversation to the amazing things you have seen or situations where you see God working. Share life experiences with each other, trials, difficulties, and challenges you're experiencing and offer to pray for each other for a set amount of time. And the next time you get together, check in. Find out how God has been working. Be devoted to fellowship that has meaning, purpose, intent, direction, encouragement, and prayer.

Third, they devoted themselves to the breaking of bread. This was commonly thought of as the Lord's Supper, although it wasn't confined to that. It was most likely done in their homes. And yes, they were devoted to it. You see, these people were so sold out to Jesus that they made the memorial of this event (the Lord's Supper) a common practice. There is something meaningful in sharing a meal together with friends. It's different than visiting over coffee. When you share a meal together, you sit long enough to let your guard down, you begin to feel comfortable enough to share a little piece of yourself with others around the table. And before you know it, you've sat at the same dining room table visiting for two or three hours.

I believe there is something even more meaningful in sharing the Sacraments together with Christian brothers and sisters. When all who gather to join in sharing the Sacraments are on the same page—broken, repentant, humbled, collectively admitting our need for a Savior—then the body of Christ is wide open to the moving of the Holy Spirit. The early Church understood this. They were like family to each other—the family of God who ate together, fellowshipped with one another, and enjoyed the Lord's Supper together. And they continued steadfastly in this practice.

And finally, as I mentioned before, *they were devoted to prayer*. Any time. Any place. They weren't confined to a certain time of day or particular place like the Jews practiced. They were simply committed to prayer. They were committed to praying together. As I said earlier, eighteen times in the book of Acts some form of the word "pray" is linked with a group or pair of people.

How many in your church are devoted to prayer? How many in your church are committed to praying together? In my experience, it's only the "faithful few" who are devoted to prayer. It's only the "faithful few" who are committed to praying together. There are many who organize, but few who agonize in prayer. Sadly, the burden of the church's effectiveness is left to the "faithful few" who are devoted to prayer. Part of the Church working right is people devoted, dedicated, and committed to praying together.

THE COMMITMENT OF THE CALLED

Are we committed to these four essentials? Or are we just committed to "extras"? Are we committed to these fundamentals or just committed to "fluff"?

This group of first-century Christians made the most of their time spent together. Their fellowship wasn't flat—it was on fire! It was exciting! It was powerful! It was amazing! And God did many amazing things in and through these folks because the Church was working right!

What happened when those first-century Christians prayed together? "The Lord added to their number daily" (Acts 2:47). Buildings shook, people were filled with the Holy Spirit, and they spoke the word of God boldly (Acts 4:31). Peter's prison chains fell off (Acts 12:7). And an earthquake occurred, opening the prison doors for Paul and Silas (Acts 16:25-26).

I don't think we realize the power God has given us in this thing called prayer. I don't think we realize or understand or grasp the power God has given us through His Holy Spirit. The same Holy Spirit that entered into these first-century Christians at Pentecost is the same Holy Spirit that dwells within us today. "And now you also have heard the truth, the Good News that God saves you. And when you believed in Christ, he identified you as his own by giving you the Holy Spirit, whom he promised long ago" (Ephesians 1:13, NLT). Shouldn't we anticipate and expect God's Spirit to move mightily when we pray now just as much as He did then?

THE POWER OF PRAYER TODAY

What happens when we 21st century Christians pray together? First of all we must understand that *praying together is a privilege.* I love King David's attitude in Psalm 122:1. He said "I rejoiced with those who said to me, 'Let us go to the house of the LORD.'" David had such anticipation and eagerness to meet in the house of the Lord. Why? Perhaps because he understood what the prophet Isaiah later proclaimed. "...these I will bring to my holy mountain and give them joy in my house of prayer. Their burnt offerings and sacrifices will be accepted on my altar; for my house will be called a house of prayer for all nations" (Isaiah 56:7). Joy in God's house of prayer! Friends, we *get* to pray together! That's exciting!

I am involved in a group called Moms In Touch (www. momsintouch.org). Perhaps you are familiar with this group. Moms In Touch International is two or more moms who meet for one hour each week to pray for their children, their schools, their teachers, and administrators.[1] I cannot express to you the joy that has been given to me by getting together with this group of women every week to pray for our children, the schools they attend, and their teachers and staff there. None of us attend the same church or even the same type of church. But our desires are the same for our kids. It is such an incredible blessing to me to get together with women of different backgrounds who believe in the same God. It is a blessing to gather together and bathe our kids, teachers, staff, bus drivers, crossing guards, etc. in prayer. It's not at all a duty that I have been called to, but a delight that I get to be a part of! Not only do we get to see the power of prayer come to life, but the bond of fellowship we have with one another is as precious to us as it is to a God who created the gift of fellowship.

Next, when we pray together we have the promise of God's presence. In Matthew 18:19-20 Jesus said, "And I tell you once more that if two of you on earth agree in asking for anything it will be granted to you by my Heavenly Father. For wherever two or three people come together in my name, I am there, right among you!" (JBP). Isn't that cool? God Himself is in our midst when we take time to pray together. We don't always acknowledge that. We aren't always aware. But He is aware of us. He delights in our gathering so much that He wants to join us. Every time. That is an incredible fact!

Third, when we pray together there is tremendous power. We saw what happened in the first century when people prayed together. Incredible, unbelievable things. Powerful things.

I don't know if you have ever been a part of a corporate prayer service for a specific need. I have. Our church has a general time of prayer every Wednesday evening. Not many people come—sadly, only a handful really. Years ago I played my guitar and we sang and worshiped before our senior pastor led our time of prayer. It was always pretty general and pretty low key. However our associate pastor's wife was suddenly struck with a life threatening illness. And on one particular Wednesday the whole church was called to come participate in prayer. The senior pastor and I had no idea how many people would be there. We hadn't really discussed the dynamics or logistics of what we would do that evening. But as it turned out the entire sanctuary was packed that evening. Our general Wednesday evening prayer service went from a few to a few hundred. God's people rallied together to bathe Ethelanne in prayer. We continued on as we usually did. I played my guitar. We sang. We worshiped. We wept. And we prayed. Not only was God's presence known that evening, His power was unleashed. You see, Ethelanne was nearing death. The family was nearing a decision to harvest her organs. But God graciously honored the corporate prayers of His people. The power of God was revealed. It was a powerful time of testimony for God's Holy Spirit in the life of our church. And Ethelanne is alive and well today. Praise God!

Finally, when we pray together we get to participate in furthering God's kingdom. Souls are won for eternity when we pray together. Lives are changed forever when we pray together. Doors are opened, barriers are broken, and the Good News of Jesus Christ is shared with someone because pockets of Christians are devoting themselves to prayer.

THE PRIVILEGE OF PRAYER TODAY

Friends, as I said before, praying together is a privilege. We *get* to enjoy God's presence. We *get* to experience and witness a power that's both amazing and humbling all at the same time. And we *get* to be a part of changing people's lives for eternity.

I agree with Bill Hybels. There's nothing like the Church when the Church is working right! There's nothing like your church when your church is working right. And praying together is a key part to the Church (and your church) working right. It is a key part to our fellowship being on fire.

What is your excuse for not praying together? Maybe it is time to face your fear. Maybe it is time to look your "verbaprayerophobia" square in the eye and say "I want to be a part of something powerful and amazing. I want to experience the joy of praying collectively with my brothers and sisters in Christ. I want to watch God go to work in the fellowship of my brothers and sisters in Christ."

You see, one of the best things about praying together is praising God together because He went to work. Rejoicing with each other, celebrating God's goodness together because you persisted in prayer together is a true gift from above.

Isn't it time to move your fellowship from *flat* to *on fire*?

MAKING IT REAL

1. Do a current inventory. Recall the last time you got together with a few of your Christian friends. What was the conversation about? Was your fellowship *flat* or *on fire*? How will you direct the conversation the next time you fellowship with other Christians?
2. Read through the book of Acts over the next couple weeks. Take note of the power of God's Holy Spirit. Take note of the devotion to prayer. Take note of how often you see people praying together. Take note of how God might be challenging you.
3. Do you realize the power God has given you through His Holy Spirit? Embrace the promise of Ephesians 1:13.
4. Try exercising that power this week by praying together with some other Christians. Pay attention to what happens next. Watch God go to work.

11

And The Answer Is . . .

Imagine for a moment that you can't stand your job. It's miserable. It's too far to drive, your boss is unreasaonable, the pay is terrible, and the benefits even worse. You're desperate for something better. *Anything* better. So, you decide to be proactive in making your employment situation better. You update your resume, comb the classifieds, make some phone calls, etc. Low and behold you come across the "perfect" job. It's the answer to all your employment woes. It's a great career opportunity for you with room for upward advancement. It's more money than you're making now, a shorter commute, and the benefits are too good to be true. You feel you are very qualified and hiring you would be a win for both you and this company. In other words, you *really* want this job. You fill out an application. You go through the interview process. Now how do you react when you don't get the job, and you find out they gave it to someone else? Angry. Crushed. Hurt. Bitter. Maybe shocked because you believed this was the perfect answer for you. Perhaps frustrated because now you'll have to start back at the proverbial square one. "I don't understand," you question. "I thought I was perfect for this job. I thought it was perfect for me."

What about this scenario—they offer you the job, but you'll have to wait six months to start it. How do you react then? Sort of excited. Confused. Impatient. Glad you got the job, but it wasn't really the time frame you were hoping for. Do you march in there and say, "I want this job and I want it right now!"? Are you willing to wait six months for this "perfect" job? Will you be able to endure your current "miserable job" and wait for the "miracle job"?

Finally, what's your reaction if they offer you the job and you start on Monday? Elated. Excited. Thankful. Grateful. Hopeful that life for you will begin to take a much needed swing upward. Chances are you want to celebrate and call everyone you know.

Three different answers to something you longed for, something you hoped for, something you thought was "right" for you. So it is with our prayers. Sometimes we get what we long for, what we hope for, what we believe is "right" for us. Sometimes we have to wait. And sometimes we flat out get rejected. The answers we receive from God can truly leave a permanent mark on us, can't they?

For ten chapters we have talked about prayer—how to pray, who to pray for, when to pray, different kinds of prayer, etc. We've looked at several prayers in Scripture. We've dissected them, broken them down, and learned a great deal about prayer. But there's one thing we haven't looked at— God's answers.

Does God *always* answer our prayers? If so, how do we react to those answers? I suppose there are various reactions to various answers based on our various personalities. We could liken it to how we react when we approach a traffic light.

TRAFFIC LIGHTS

Do you ever catch yourself talking to the traffic lights when you're driving around town? You know . . . "C'mon green, c'mon green!" My sons will sometimes chant in the back seat with their fists pumping. "Green . . . Green . . . Green!" Or when you're approaching a light that's been green for a while you say something like, "Don't turn yellow, don't turn yellow!"

When you come to a traffic light there are three possibilities which invoke three different responses from us. (And no, talking to the light is not one of the responses.) There is the dreaded RED light at which we must stop. There is no "inching" through. We cannot proceed at our own leisure. We have to come to a complete stop.

There is the all-too-confusing YELLOW light at which we could go or we could stop. We slow down, we use caution, and we look at all other directions of traffic. Sometimes we then feel it best to stop. And other times we "floor it." I once had a friend who couldn't make up her mind at the yellow light, so she hit the gas, then the brake, then the gas, then the brake... She did this all the way through the yellow light. Unfortunately, the policeman behind her didn't appreciate that and she got a ticket for "indecision at a yellow light." Ultimately the yellow light is communicating to us to use extreme caution.

Then there's our best friend — the GREEN light. We love this guy. Green means go. Go forward. Keep on going. All lanes are clear for us. Go! Go! Go!

Just like the traffic light has three possibilities and three different responses, in the most general sense, I believe there are three ways in which God answers prayer. These answers invoke three different responses from us.

RED LIGHTS

And the answer is . . . NO! No matter how spiritual you may be, there are going to be times when God says "no" to your requests. It doesn't matter what you've sacrificed, endured, accomplished or given for the cause of Christ, God will at times deny us what we're praying for. And when this happens it can leave us angry, crushed, hurt, and even bitter. It frustrates us because we sometimes think that the answer we expect is a win-win-win. It appears to you that this particular answer to prayer would be a win for you, a win for God, and a win for the circumstance or people surrounding the circumstance. We don't understand God's "no." And sometimes it even causes us to question God, His strength, His love, His power, or even His existence. Why does God sometimes say "no"?

God sometimes says "no" because of sin in our lives. The Psalmist said "If I had cherished sin in my heart, the Lord would not have listened" (Psalm 66:18). These words are recorded in the gospel of John: "We all know that God does not listen to sinners; but He listens to anyone who worships and obeys Him" (John 9:31, NCV). Proverbs 28:9 reads "If you refuse to obey what you've been taught, your prayers will not be heard" (NCV). If we are living in disobedience to God, if we have some harbored sin, some unconfessed sin in our lives these verses suggest that God won't even hear us. This does not indicate that our perfection is a prerequisite to prayer. Besides I can't even remember or recall every time I've sinned. I think the key here is attitude and intent toward our sinfulness and our prayers. If we fully intend to keep going back to our sinful behavior as soon as we get off our knees, I'm not sure God will listen to our prayers. I would imagine God saying to us, "If you're not going to honor My request of living holy lives, why should I honor your request?" OUCH!

God can also say "no" because of our wrong motive. If our motives are self-serving, materialistic, convenience-minded, etc. God probably won't honor those. James would agree: "When you ask, you do not receive, because you ask with wrong motives, that you may spend what you get on your pleasures" (James 4:3). If we seek the things of this world, if we seek personal satisfaction or gratification God justly denies our requests.

He may also deny us when our relationships are not right. Remember what Jesus said in the Sermon on the Mount, "So if you are standing before the altar in the Temple, offering a sacrifice to God, and you suddenly remember that someone has something against you, leave your sacrifice there beside the altar. Go and be reconciled to that person. Then come and offer your sacrifice to God" (Matthew 5:23-24, NLT). We sometimes have bitterness or anger or envy toward another person, and yet we have the nerve to go before God and praise Him as if our hearts were as pure as gold. Jesus said to go and settle the score, then come and settle up with God.

Similarly, hear the words of Peter: "Husbands, in the same way be considerate as you live with your wives, and treat them with respect as the weaker partner and as heirs with you of the gracious gift of life, so that nothing will hinder your prayers" (1 Peter 3:7). Although Peter is speaking directly to husbands and wives here, I believe that it holds true with relationships in general. If we are not treating each other as we ought to, then perhaps our prayers are indeed being hindered.

Another reason why God may say "no" is for our own protection. Let's go back to the example from the beginning of this chapter. Let's say you applied for this wonderful job that you really wanted and thought was perfect for you. You didn't get the job. You're angry. You're frustrated. You're crushed. But God was actually protecting you in this situation because the company you applied to was called Enron. You had no idea that a year later that company would be splashed all over every news headline worldwide. God at work. Protecting you. Sometimes it takes a long look back to be able to see His hand of protection on us in those "red light" prayers.

Sometimes God says "no" to our requests because He has something better in mind. Remember the story of Lazarus in John 11? Remember how sisters Mary and Martha had sent a message to the Lord telling Him that their brother Lazarus was sick? They expected Him to come. They expected Him to answer their plea. After all they were dear friends with Jesus. But their request was denied and Lazarus died.

If we stopped right there it would be a hard, sad, tragic ending. However, the beauty of this story is that it didn't end with hearts left empty and hurting by a request denied. Indeed it was a "no" from God. But that's because He had something better in mind. Instead of coming to Lazarus' side and healing him while he was sick, God decided to do something far greater. Far better. Beyond what Mary and Martha were expecting. God decided to *allow* Lazarus' death so that He could raise him four days later. Amazing, isn't it? He closes one door so that beyond it He can open another one that is "immeasurably more than we can ask or imagine" (Ephesians 3:20). Cool!

Finally, God says "no" because it simply does not align with His will. Occasionally, there seems to us to be no earthly rhyme or reason why we are denied a certain request. As a matter of fact, we go back through the reasons God says "no" and we can check them off as accomplishments. We're not harboring any sin, our motives are right, our relationships are all in check, but still He says "no." Perhaps it's because it's just simply not what He wants for us. In these times we must simply remember that He's God and we aren't! We must remember that "The LORD says: My thoughts and my ways are not like yours. Just as the heavens are higher than the earth, my thoughts and my ways are higher than yours" (Isaiah 55:8-9, CEV).

As we discussed earlier when we approach a red light, it invokes a certain response from us. How then do we respond to a "no" from God? How do we react? What should the appropriate response be?

Unfortunately for some, when God says "no" they just stop believing in Him. There is a scene in the movie *The Santa Clause* (starring Tim Allen) in which two adults are sitting outside a courtroom awaiting a custody decision from the judge inside. They are reminiscing about when they stopped believing in Santa Claus. The reason wasn't because they outgrew believing. It wasn't because someone spilled the beans and told them it was all a big hoax. The reason they stopped believing in Santa Claus was that they didn't get what they longed for. Santa didn't come through on the one "special" toy they had asked for—the one game that they thought would bring ultimate joy into their world. All the prior years of believing, all the hoping, all the antici- pating . . . gone! Snatched away! Down the tubes! So they stopped believing. And for some people, this same reaction holds true when they don't get what they want from God. If every Christian stopped believing in God every time He said "no" to one of our prayers, the world wouldn't have a single Christian in it. So how, then, should we respond when God says "no"?

RED LIGHT RESPONSES

First, we need to understand that the "no" is a gift from God. Whether we like it or not, the "no" is indeed an answer from God. It's not the answer we wanted or needed or spent hours upon hours praying for. But it's an answer.

Thank Him for the "no." Yes, that's what I said. Thank Him for the "no." It may be hard. It may be painful. It may not even make sense to do so. But it is a gift from God. He may have other things in mind for us. We need to truly embrace the fact that God is sovereign. Sometimes that's comforting. Sometimes it's scary. But if we are to trust Him with our every need then we must trust Him when He says "no" as well.

I have a friend at our church who has struggled for the last several years with headaches. He's been to several specialists around Kansas City and around the nation. Lots of folks in our church have spent many hours praying for him. To date Mike has not found any relief. But he would be the first to tell you that because of God's "no" in this situation, Mike has drawn ever closer to Jesus Christ. Because of God's "no," his faith has increased not decreased. He hasn't stopped believing in God. No, actually quite the opposite. His walk with the Lord has gotten deeper and more intimate during these years of struggle.

Another response when God says "no" is that we might need to change the request. You see, when God says "no" it affords us the opportunity to rethink what we are asking. While we rethink the request I believe He enlightens us and speaks deeply within us. Upon His enlightenment we begin to pray a little differently.

I heard someone once say "let us not pray for lighter burdens but for stronger backs." That's a change of request. That's a different attitude and perspective on the situation which allows us to then "tweak" our request. Many times when we end up changing our request to God, He ends up changing us in the process.

If after we've prayed and prayed and prayed and God still is saying "no," it may be time to let it go. As a mom I see this all the time. My sons will constantly ask a question that

I constantly say "no" to, yet they keep on asking. Eventually they catch on and let go of the request.

Jesus taught a parable in Luke 18 concerning a persistent widow who kept going to the judge with her plea. The judge finally granted her request because of her persistence. Jesus' point in teaching this parable was to communicate that we should always pray and not give up. However, sometimes the requests we bring before God are simply closed doors. It's just not going to happen. This is where God's "no" means "no." And even our persistence won't change His mind. So our response then is to simply let it go because once again He's God and we aren't.

One final response when God says "no" is to ask Him how we need to grow. God said "no" for a reason. If you're anything like me you want to know *why*. Ask Him. Ask Him how you can grow through the "no." Ask God to make clear to you why He didn't honor your request. You just might be amazed at what God shows you if you're truly open to embrace His response.

YELLOW LIGHTS

And the answer is . . . SLOW! Those crazy yellow lights. Sometimes they can be just as bad as the red ones. To me, they are always based on a timing issue. If I would have gone faster a block earlier I would have hit the green light. If I would have gone slower a mile back I would have hit the green light. It's timing. And you know what they say . . . timing is everything.

We don't like to wait. It's frustrating to have to wait. I waited in line at the pharmacy for 40 minutes last week. It was very frustrating to say the least. I had been told an hour and a half earlier that my prescription would be ready in twenty minutes. I was generous and gave them ninety minutes. But then I had to wait forty more. I didn't care for that at all. It made me want to change pharmacies. (Thankfully, I never think of changing "gods" when I have to wait on our God.)

So why does God say "wait"? Why does God say "not yet"? It all boils down to timing. It's just the wrong timing. It's wrong timing for you, wrong timing for the situation, wrong timing for those people you're praying for, etc. Something or someone is not ready.

It is essential for us to remember that God will reveal Himself to us on His time table not on ours. And quite frankly sometimes that just stinks. We don't like to wait for the healing—we want it now. We don't like to wait for His provision—we need financial relief now. Waiting stinks. Waiting is painful. Waiting can be so defeating. How then should we respond?

YELLOW LIGHT RESPONSES

First we need to understand that the "slow" is a gift from God. Whether we like it or not, the "slow" is indeed an answer from God. It's not the answer we wanted or needed or spent hours upon hours praying for. But it's an answer.

Thank Him for the "slow." Yes, that's what I said. Thank Him for the "slow." It may be hard. It may be painful. It may not even make sense to do so. But it is a gift from God. Remember something or someone is not ready yet. Remember that God is in charge and we're not. Remember He will reveal Himself. But we might have to wait.

Another response during the "slow" is to consider God's faithfulness in the past. Spend some time recalling how God has blessed you, taken care of you, protected you, provided for you, etc. You see, the "slow" doesn't mean God has abandoned you. It doesn't mean He's not present. It doesn't mean He's gone on vacation and left you standing there to fend for yourself. He is still a loving, gracious, and awesome God.

And that's precisely what we need to consider from our past experiences.

Consider God's promises for the future as well. Standing on God's promises for the future is powerful. Promises like "I can do all things through Christ who strengthens me" (Philippians 4:13, NKJV). Or perhaps "'For I know the plans I have for you,' declares the LORD, 'plans to prosper you and not to harm you, plans to give you hope and a future'" (Jeremiah 29:11). We can still rest upon His promises even when we're waiting on God for an answer.

Another way to respond when God says "slow" is to "P.U.S.H." — Pray Until Something Happens. Please don't misunderstand me here. I'm not talking about the kicking, screaming, moaning, groaning, whining, and complaining kind of praying until you get your way. I'm talking about praying through the "slow" until something happens. Pray until God changes the situation or until God changes you.

It is highly possible that God may want to develop some character trait in you like endurance, patience, trust, etc. He might be challenging you in your pride or submission, for instance. But if you give up praying during this "slow" period, you'll never find out what God wants you to learn! So, persevere. Pray until something happens.

Finally, when God says "slow," we need to focus on God's grace and power. Do you remember when Paul was given the thorn in his flesh in 2 Corinthians 12? Paul recorded that three times he pleaded with the Lord to take it away from him. Do you remember God's answer? God said, "My grace is sufficient for you, for my power is made perfect in weakness" (2 Corinthians 12:9). Now if I were Paul I'd be thinking, "Big deal! I don't need grace. I need an answer!" But this *was* an answer! God indeed carried Paul through. His power was made perfect in Paul's weakness, not Paul's strength. When God allows us the privilege of waiting we sometimes become weak. And it is during these times when His strength can be manifested in our weaknesses.

GREEN LIGHTS

And the answer is . . . GO! You know that feeling you get when you cruise down a busy street and every traffic signal you come to is green? Man, is that cool or what? Every light green! You almost can't believe your good fortune. You're wondering what you did to deserve a gift like that while you hold your private celebration in your car.

When God says "yes" to our prayers we celebrate. We sometimes can't believe our good fortune. We wonder what we did to deserve that. Why *does* He say "yes"?

God says "yes" because the timing is right, our motive is right, and we are right in our relationship with Him. God desires to bless His children. You matter to Him. He wants to meet your need and fulfill your desires. God is not some angry judge ready to settle your case with a swing of His gavel. He is a Father. He wants us to crawl up in His lap where He can bless us and give us the desires of our hearts.

GREEN LIGHT RESPONSES

How then should we respond? Once again . . . the "go" is a gift from God. *Thank Him for the "go!"* It is an answer. It is a wonderful answer.

Celebrate! Don't celebrate the answer. Celebrate God! Do you remember how King David celebrated when the Ark of the Covenant was finally brought back to Jerusalem in 2 Samuel 6? He danced and leaped before the Lord. He didn't care that his wife Michal was disgusted by it. He celebrated before the Lord. Don't be afraid to celebrate God in a passionate, jubilant way. After all, when David's wife questioned his celebratory praise, he responded by saying, "I will become even more undignified than this..." (2 Samuel 6:22).

Finally, when God says "yes," share your victory experience with others. Sharing your answered prayers is a faith builder for others. It is exciting to be able to rejoice with our brothers and sisters in Christ when God goes to work in our lives. It also causes the ears of those non-Christians in your midst to perk up when you talk about God answering your prayers. What a witness we can be for our Lord when our Lord goes to work for us!

You see, friends, no matter how God chooses to answer us, He is working. He is working even now as you read this book. We often don't know it or don't see it, but God is faithfully working in the lives of His children 24/7. That's just the kind of God He is.

Red lights, green lights, and yellow lights—they are an everyday occurrence as we journey through our city streets and towns. They are an everyday occurrence as we journey through this thing called the Christian life. God provides answers. But remember, in order to get an answer we have to be praying first. So, begin the journey. And please . . . pay attention to the traffic lights!

MAKING IT REAL

1. How do you respond when God says "no" to your prayer request? Do you question God? Remember to trust Him completely. He has your best interest at heart.

2. How do you react when God says "slow"? Do you try to make Him go faster? Do you get busier trying to force an answer? Let God be God. Patiently let Him work. Ask Him for endurance while you wait.

3. When was the last time God said "yes" to one of your prayers? And how did you react? Remember to cele-

brate! Share that victory with your brothers and sisters in Christ. Even share it with those non-Christians around you. You never know where bragging on our awesome God will take you with your non-Christian friends.

4. How are you growing spiritually through God's answers? If you don't know, ask Him to enlighten you.

12

What's The Big Deal?

So, what's the big deal? What *does* prayer have to do with anything? Does it really matter that much to the average Christian?

In the first chapter of this book I told you what Richard Foster had to say about prayer. Let me remind you: "Of all the Spiritual Disciplines prayer is the most central because it ushers us into perpetual communion with the Father. Real prayer is life creating and life changing."

I truly believe that prayer is life creating and life changing. I've seen it. I've witnessed it. I've been a part of it. Unfortunately, many Christians today aren't experiencing anything close. I believe there are two elements that stand in the way of our experiencing life creating, life changing prayer.

PLAYING IT SAFE

The first is what I refer to as "Safe Mode Syndrome." Sometimes we pray in total safe mode. We pray hesitantly. We waffle. We hem and haw. We pray indecisively as if we can't really make up our minds what we want. For instance,

when we have a sick friend our prayers may sound something like this: "God, I pray that You would heal Tracy. You
don't have to if You don't want to. But I'd like You to. And
Tracy would like to be healed. But it's okay if You don't
want her to be healed. But it sure would be nice if she was
healed. So please heal her. Or make her better. Yeah, make
her better if that's okay with You. . ."

When we pray like this—tentatively and half hoping—I
think God is up there scratching His head thinking, "I haven't
the foggiest idea how to answer that prayer." We play it all
too safe. We're afraid of "going out on a limb" in our prayers.
I mean, what if God doesn't honor those "limb prayers"? Ah,
but what if He does?

Yes, I realize that ultimately we have to submit to the
will of God in our prayers. We discussed surrendering our
will to God's will in Chapter 2. I completely understand and
embrace that fact. But when we pray in safe mode, where is
the faith in praying this way? Where is the radical belief and
trust in the Almighty God?

Consider Peter when he prayed in Acts 3:6. On the way
to the temple, he met a crippled beggar. Peter looked right
at him and said, "In the name of Jesus Christ of Nazareth,
walk." No hemming and hawing. No playing it safe. No
waffling back and forth on whether or not this man should
receive a healing. It was just bold and faith-filled prayer.

Or take a look at any of Paul's prayers. He didn't pray
indecisively or hesitantly. He didn't waver in his prayers for
the Colossians or the Philippians as if he wasn't quite sure
what he wanted for them. No, he prayed audaciously and
with much conviction. He not only prayed this way, but he
lived his life this way.

Will God honor our prayers every time we pray boldly
and with radical faith? If He chooses to, He will. But how
can He begin to give us the desires of our hearts when we

aren't even sure what we want? How can He answer when we pray so tentatively and timidly?

Don't let "Safe Mode Syndrome" get in the way of life creating, life changing prayer for you. Move beyond indecisiveness in your prayers. Step out past the vacillating, wavering, and uncertain style of prayer. Go out on a limb. Pray boldly. And be prepared to be amazed at our incredible loving God!

PLEASURE IN THE PROCESS

The second stumbling block to life creating, life changing prayer is something called "Destination Disease." This kind of prayer is more concerned with getting to the destination than finding joy in the journey.

Think about taking a vacation. You plan and save and make all the appropriate arrangements. The time has come to embark on your trip. It's about a six-hour drive to your desired destination. If the final destination is all you think about, you'll miss out on the beautiful scenery on the drive. You'll miss out on valuable relationship time with those in the car (a perfect opportunity for some fellowship on fire). The journey will be miserable for you (and everyone else in the car) because all you can think about is getting there.

But if you choose to enjoy every moment of the trip, the destination is even sweeter once it arrives. You will see things you have never seen before. You will learn new things about the people you are riding with. You will smile more and laugh more. You'll bless more and be more blessed. You will have wonderful memories to share about the trip you took to get to the destination.

So it is with prayer. When we pray through something vitally important to us, we need to pay attention to the journey. Don't miss the journey because your eyes are focused only on the answer to your prayer. God wants to show us the scenery of our hearts as we travel. God wants us to learn new things. He wants us to enjoy Him. While we progress, He wants us to bless His heart while He blesses ours. He also wants to build in us precious memories of the journey to share with others. And when we reach our destination—when the answer finally comes to fruition—how sweet it is!

Don't let things like "Safe Mode Syndrome" and "Destination Disease" steal from your prayer life. Experience all there is to an abundant life of prayer.

REVISITING THE PRIVILEGE

Do you remember how I defined prayer? Prayer is the privilege we have to draw near to the heart of God—both speaking to and hearing from our gracious Heavenly Father. I hope that along this journey you have learned something about this *privilege* God has given us. And yes, this privilege is indeed a BIG DEAL! As we have seen in the Scripture passages we looked at throughout this book, God revealed Himself in magnificent ways all because of the privilege of drawing near to the heart of God—all because people prayed.

If this privilege were nonexistent, we as Christians wouldn't even be able to know this great God of ours. Our relationship with Him would solely be based upon what we read in the pages of Scripture. Think about it . . . if you could not communicate in any way with someone you loved and they couldn't communicate with you, what kind of relationship would that be? A silent one! A cold one! A dead one!

I'm so thankful that the privilege of prayer does exist. But for many Christians today, prayer is far too neglected. It's a Christian discipline that's hardly practiced. It's essential, but essentially ignored. I hope this book has changed (or will change) some of that.

We were created to be in fellowship with our loving Father. Intimate, wonderful fellowship with Him. We were created to communicate with God and He with us. Friends, we *get* to do this very thing through the privilege of prayer. It is indeed a BIG DEAL!

I have a friend who is always verbalizing her desire or need to start a new discipline, behavior, change in her life, etc. There is always something she is going to begin working on or implementing. But it's mostly talk. Seeing the aspirations without the action, a wise older woman in her church approached her and said something like, "You're always talking about starting these new changes in your life. But you never act upon them. Don't talk about it—be about it!"

She shared that story with me and I absolutely loved it. Not only did I love the illustration, but I loved the phrase. *Don't talk about it—be about it!* And it absolutely applies right here and now. Don't talk about becoming a man or woman of prayer. *Be* a man or woman of prayer. From here forward, make it happen. *Be* in close relationship with our Heavenly Father. *Be* in conversation with the God who created you. *Be* in fellowship with the One who hung each and every star in the sky. *Be* in communion with the Almighty! One more time . . . don't talk about it—be about it!

I want you to know that each and every one of you holding this book in your hands right now has been bathed in prayer by me and a host of my prayer warrior friends and family members. We have prayed that this book would in fact be a journey for you—a journey through Scripture, a journey of faith, a journey of visible spiritual growth.

Please know that I continue to pray for you . . . I pray for you now.

I pray that God would draw near to you—that His presence would envelop you. I pray that you would be able to see Him at work in your life and in the lives of those around you. I pray that in your own spiritual walk with the Lord you would be encouraged—that your heart and mind would be touched in some special way by our Heavenly Father. I pray that you would have the strength and courage to pray for yourself, pray for friends and family, and pray for folks you don't even know. I pray that you would have the faith to pray out loud with the body of Christ. And I pray that you would hunger and thirst for more of God in your life. Seek Him. Seek His face always. And I pray that God would pour out His blessing on each and every one of you! Enjoy the journey, my friends.

In the powerful, powerful name of Jesus, AMEN!

Notes

Chapter 1

1. "Gandhi Quotes": http://www.happypublishing.com/ quotations/gandhi_quotes.html. Accessed February 20, 2008.
2. Reprinted by permission. *Strengthening Your Grip*, Charles R. Swindoll, 1982, 1998, Thomas Nelson Inc., Nashville, TN, 142. All rights reserved.
3. Richard Foster, *Celebration of Discipline: The Path to Spiritual Growth*, New York, NY, 1998, HarperCollins, 33, Reprinted by permission of HarperCollins Publishers.
4. Stormie Omartian, *The Power of a Praying® Parent*, Eugene, OR, 1995, Harvest House, 18, Used by permission.
5. Rick Warren, *The Purpose Driven Life*, Grand Rapids, MI, 2002, Zondervan, 17.
6. Bill Hybels, *Too Busy Not to Pray*, Downers Grove, IL, 1998, InterVarsity Press, 125.
7. Reprinted by permission. *Intimacy with the Almighty*, Charles R. Swindoll, 1996, Thomas Nelson Inc., Nashville, TN, 26. All rights reserved.

Chapter 2

1. http://www.signonsandiego.com/uniontrib/20050626
   /news_1c26conside.html,
   Accessed March 10, 2008, Newshouse News Service,
   2005, Used by permission.
2. http://flighttraining.aopa.org/learntofly/project_
   pilot/articles/0206article_pf.html, Accessed March
   10, 2008, Aircraft Owners and Pilots Association,
   1999-2004.

Chapter 3

1. Taken from *In The Presence of My Enemies* by Gracia
   Burnham with Dean Merrill. Copyright © 2003 by
   Tyndale House Publishers. Used by permission of
   Tyndale House Publishers, Inc. All rights reserved.
2. http://www.desiringgod.org/ResourceLibrary/
   Sermons/ByDate/1992/801_The_Echo_and_
   Insufficiency_of_Hell_Part_2/, Accessed February 6,
   2008, By John Piper. © Desiring God. Website: desir-
   ingGod.org.
3. Jakob Grimm, *Grimms' Fairy Tales*, Cleveland, OH,
   1947, World Publishing Company, 332-3.
4. IBID, 333.

Chapter 4

1. Richard Foster, *Celebration of Discipline: The
   Path to Spiritual Growth*, New York, NY, 1998,
   HarperCollins, 54, Reprinted by permission of
   HarperCollins Publishers.
2. IBID, 60.

Chapter 7

1. John Ortberg, *God Is Closer Than You Think*, Grand
   Rapids, MI, 2005, Zondervan, 161.

Chapter 9
1. Hannah Whitall Smith, *The Christian's Secret of a Happy Life*, copyright 1998, Bridge Logos Publishers, 104.

Chapter 10
1. http://www.momsintouch.org/NewDesign/aboutus. html. Accessed January 17, 2008.

Acknowledgements

†

I always thank God for all of you and pray for you
constantly. As I pray to our God and Father about you,
I think of your faithful work, your loving deeds, and the
enduring hope you have because of our Lord Jesus Christ.
(Adapted from 1 Thessalonians 1:2-3, New Living Translation)

I am truly thankful for many people in my life. I'm very blessed to have the circle of family and friends around me that I have. God is incredibly good.

I'd like to thank my wonderful parents, Bill and Binny Pearce. Thank you so much for all the love, support, encouragement, and prayers. Thanks for modeling what it means to be fully devoted followers of Christ.

My gratitude goes to Dr. Lonni Pearce for the hours of reading, editing, great insight, encouragement, and prayers. What a blessing you are to me and our family.

Thanks to Kari Perry for all my graphics needs. Your creativity blows me away! I appreciate the time and effort you put into your work. What a gift you have!

Thanks to my dear friend April Downey. I couldn't have done this without you—literally. You are a blessing, a delight, and a gift from God.

Many thanks to my prayer warrior friends: Jan, AJ, Chelle, Amy, Ed, Ape, Robin, Michelle, Mark, and Therese.

You all bless my heart so much. Your willingness to lift me to the throne of grace is humbling to say the least. What a privilege to have my brothers and sisters in Christ interceding for me.

To Matt, Caleb, and Quinn—my three special guys. Thanks . . . and I love you!

Printed in the United States
132338LV00003B/3/P